Love, Hope and Comfort

Wisdom in Experience

By
Lisa Wake

Grosvenor House
Publishing Limited

All rights reserved
Copyright © Lisa Wake, 2023

The right of Lisa Wake to be identified as the author of this
work has been asserted in accordance with Section 78
of the Copyright, Designs and Patents Act 1988

The book cover is copyright to Lisa Wake

This book is published by
Grosvenor House Publishing Ltd
Link House
140 The Broadway, Tolworth, Surrey, KT6 7HT.
www.grosvenorhousepublishing.co.uk

This book is sold subject to the conditions that it shall not, by way of
trade or otherwise, be lent, resold, hired out or otherwise circulated
without the author's or publisher's prior consent in any form of
binding or cover other than that in which it is published and
without a similar condition including this condition being
imposed on the subsequent purchaser.

A CIP record for this book
is available from the British Library

ISBN 978-1-80381-504-6

Acknowledgements

I would like to acknowledge my husband, Simon, for the help and support he has given over the last five months due to my mental health.

The support of my three children, Thomas, Amy, and Patrick. I am blessed and honoured to be their mum, and nan to my grandson, Finley. They give me encouragement and wise advice.

Friends, past and present, for their wise words, encouragement, support, and help. Thank you Sue, Sheryl, Alma, Tamry & Sue, and Pete.

To my work colleagues at Empowering U for their patience, support, and help over recent months/years, and to my family – Mum, Dad, sisters, brother, uncles, aunts, who are here, and nans and grandads, all unfortunately no longer here.

Thank you to you all, you are all super amazing, super incredible.

Thank you xxxx

Dedication

The dedication of my poems not only goes to my friends, family, and loved ones, past and present, but to all who have their own trials they are facing in life, be it physical, mental, emotional, or otherwise. May hope and comfort be provided with love in the poems you read, helping you gain the strength to move forward.

Love to all xxxx

About the author

Lisa is the eldest of six children – four sisters, one brother. She has three children – two boys, and one girl – and one grandson, all of whom she adores very much. She is a care and support worker. She has experienced many trials, especially mental health. She believes everyone is equal, we are all special and unique individuals, and should be treated fairly as such.

The poems in this book she has written in her spare time – poems that have uplifted her, inspired her, and comforted her. Lisa loves to help others and feels that her poems will do just that, by expressing her hope, love, and faith, to help others by guiding with the wisdom she has gained with her experiences in her life. She hopes that whoever reads the poems will not only enjoy reading them, but will also feel the help and guidance from her wisdom.

Contents

Part 1 – Spiritual Uplift 1
   I am here 3
   You're my Inspiration 4
   In God's Hands 5
   The Angel Speaks 6
   Go and know Him 7
   Turn to Him 8
   He's calling to you 9
   Confidence 10
   Missionaries 11
   Choose the Right 12
   Faith 13
   Ark 14
   Thank you dear Father 15
   Prayer of Redemption 16
   Our Saviour, the King 17
   S.M.I.L.E. 18
   Hope 19
   Afflictions 20
   Bearing your Testimony 21
   The Lord 22
   Holy Spirit 23

Part 2 – Love 25
   I'm Missing you 27
   I Smile 28
   I long for you 29
   If I Could 30
   Your Smile 31
   You touch me 32

I think about you 33
From my Heart, to your Heart 34
The One 35
My Busy Bee 36
We may not be Together 37
King of my Heart 38
Though you're not here 39
I wait for you 40
Heart of Gold 41
That Special Person 42
A Valentine's Love 43
All you need in Life 44
You are a Blessing 45
I'd Love to Feel 46
Beauty of our Love 47
Eternally you and me 48
You and me 49
Love so True 50
My Valentine Just for you 51
Valentine 52
Love 53
Be with Someone 54
If you Chance to Meet a Guy 55
Precious Rose 56
Another you 57
Into the Universe 58
L is for.. 59
Part 3 – Hope 61
Hope 63
Positive Energy 64
Your Beauty Within 65

LOVE, HOPE AND COMFORT: WISDOM IN WITH EXPERIENCE

Support, in your Hour of Need 66
Words of Comfort (revised) 67
Don't give up 68
Never Lose Hope 69
Dreams 70
Sense of Humour 71
Happiness 72
The Hero Within 73
Smiles Through Nerves 74
Be Not Afraid 75

Part 4 – Inspirational and Special People 77
Chuck Norris 79
Thomas 80
Love, Hope, and Faith 81
Amy 82
Beautiful Angel 83
Finley 84
Patrick 85
Just for you 86
Our Children 87
Simon 88
Stephanie 89
Love Renewed, Blessings Shared 90
Nan 91
A Snowflake in our Hearts 92
Grandparents 93
Dad 94
Mum 95
Sheryl 96
Alma 97
Sue 98

A Mum to One and All	99
Tamry	100
Kat	101
Jacob	102
Part 5 – Nature	**103**
I Hear Nature Calling Me	105
Stars Twinkling Up High	106
Hello, Nature, Hello	107
I whispered	108
In the Lockdown	109
Seasons of the Year	110
The Rainbow	111
Nature, Beautiful Nature	112
The Colours of Life	113
Magpies	114
Snow	115
Dreams	116
The Beauty of Living	117
Daisy	118
I want to go	119
The Shadow	120
This Life a Gift	121
Hello	122
Butterfly	123
Clear Night Sky	124
Part 6 – Precious Moments	**125**
Remember Me	127
A Baby's Laugh	128
A Lost Angel	129
Wedding Day	130
Birth of a Daughter	131

LOVE, HOPE AND COMFORT: WISDOM IN WITH EXPERIENCE

Birth of a Son 132
Birthdays 133
To Become a Nan 134
A Mother 135
My Heart 136
As I Lay 137
Part 7 – Thoughts, Feelings, and Experiences 139
My Little Angels, I'm So Sorry 141
Experiences 142
If I Can't 143
We're Only Human 144
Hearts in Pain 145
Anxiety and Depression 146
Post-traumatic Stress Disorder (PTSD) 147
When is This Trial Going to End 148
Hip, Hip, Yay 149
My Life 150
The Metaphor 151
A Banana 152
Frightened 153
A Broken Heart 154
Forgiveness 155
Soul-searching 156
Poverty 157
Stronger than Life 158
The Negative Life 159
Fantasies 160
Feeling Alone 161
Grass is Greener 162
Be Careful What You Wish For 163
It's Not Your Fault 164

Look for the Hero	165
Cancer	166
Homeless	167
I Used to be Frightened	168
I Remember When	169
Anger	170
The Poem of Love	171

Part 8 – Inspirational 173

Inspiration	175
You are Blessed	176
Talents	177
Bonfire Night	178
The Two Wolves	179
I Started Reading a Book Today	180
Merry Christmas	181
Racism	182
Happy New Year	183
Christmas	184
Easter	185
Thank You	186
Football	187
Charity	188
Happiness is	189
Let Your Inner Child Out	190
Individual Happiness	191
Lisa	192
Words of Comfort	193
Paradise is Not a Place	194
An Old Man Staring Back at Me	195
Man in the Moon	196

Part 9 – Personal and Favourites Written 197
   Unique Me Unique You..199
   What Christmas Means to Me 200
   Ireland..201
   An Irish..202
   I'd Rather be in Ireland 203
   My Children Mean the Universe to Me 204
   Hope 205

Part 1 – Spiritual Uplift

I am here

I am here
I'm not far
Smiling down, on you
Look to the stars
I'm shining bright
For you to see
Dear sons and daughters
It is me
In your hearts
I shall stay
In the wind, blowing
So you feel me, today
I'm your dad
And I love you, true
Never to leave your side
Always with you
At night, when I shine
Just look up, and say good night

2nd March 2020

You're my Inspiration

You're my inspiration
The light, you give to me
'Tis the inspiration, that I need
Helping me to see

You're my inspiration
The gift to help me endure
No matter, how much I struggle
I know you're there, for sure

You're my inspiration
That is what you are
No matter, how tired I get
You're definitely my star

You're my inspiration
The poems, that I write
Ideas, that come, from afar
Cherished, with the light

You're my inspiration
The warmth, I do feel
Happiness in writing
And joy, to help heal

You're my inspiration
The want, to share
Comes with no cost
But with love and care

You're my inspiration
Experiences I've had
Words of advice shared with you
Wisdom in your hand

18th/19th May 2022

In God's Hands

Embrace with grace
Your trials, and tribulations
Call upon, your Father in heaven
To help you through, with patience
The blessings, that come to
Enduring your trials,
Diligently seeking, going for miles
Although at the time, your trials
Seem too much to bear
Ask for our Lord, and he will be there
To guide us through, and show us the way
Helping us smile, through each brand new day
In God's hands, we are held
We, our Father's children, are comforted

16th March 2019

The Angel Speaks

When the angel speaks to you
Calling out the number two
It's a message from above
To have faith, never give up
Never lose hope
Believe in you
Guardian angels and number two
Be open to them, as they are near
Helping you have no fear
A message of hope and inspiration
Keeping up harmony and motivation
An angel's patience and affection
Sharing their love and compassion
To help you with goals and dreams
Creating balance and peace
Angels support you in your trials
Heavenly Father tests your dials
To see your reaction, what you do
How you cope and get through
Have faith, appreciate yourself
Be kind and celebrate life, and love
So when angels say number two
Remember they're near and speaking to you
To support and help you through
A message of hope in all you do

16th December 2022

Go and know Him

Go and know Him, who knows us well
To reach out, and help us dwell
Go and hear Him, who guides us today
To choose the right, not fade away
God and love Him, who loves us for sure
Giving mercy, that we may endure
Go and serve Him. As he had done, now
He is teaching, and showing us how
Go to Him, who sacrificed his life
That we may repent, when we, take a dive
Go to Him, who never gives up on us
His love so pure, he gives, freely with trust
Heavenly Father, saviour too
Their love, will see us through

6th April 2021

Turn to Him

Turn to Him, that gives you breath
That gives you light, that gives you strength

Turn to Him, that gives you hope
That gives you peace, that you may cope

Turn to Him, that gives you wisdom
That gives you knowledge, from His kingdom

Turn to Him, that gives you grace
And has mercy, to put redemption in place

Turn to Him, that gives you love
That gives you joy, and laughter from above

Turn to Him, when feeling weak, or feeling low
Talk to Him and He will show

The path for you, to directly take
Step by step, you will make

Turn to Him, when your soul is weary
Dear Father in heaven, I now can see clearly

2nd November 2017
Inspired by the talk, "A yearning for home" by Dieter F. Uchtdorf, 2nd councillor in 1st presidency, October 2017, General Conference

He's calling to you

He's calling to you
He's reaching for you
To put your hands in His
He wants to help you, find your way
Through each night, and each day

Our Father in heaven, brother too
They're reaching, to let you know
They are both, by your side
Wherever you may go
You don't have to hide

He's calling you
To turn to Him
When feeling, weak and weary
Hold the rod, and talk to Him
And He will, guide you clearly

2nd March 2020

Confidence

Christ, the heavenly Father's Son
Only one, to treasure near and far
Never forgetting, the holy one's commands
Faith and forever believing
Indecisions made better by prayer
Deliverance from evil, with guidance of the Holy Spirit
Eternal Life and all that comes within it
Never failing to keep His promises
Confirming into the church
Enduring to the end, a celestial paradise to meet again

2007/2008

Missionaries

Come down from up above
Sent to us, with love, as pure as a dove
Working hard to help you and me
To convert to a place, we will see
They are angels in disguise
Just as happy, as the sunrise
They all show, unto us, their smiles
Helping those who are in need
Very spiritual they are indeed
Called of God to spread the word
With faith and hope, they are heard
In all weather, the friendly bunch bring
On their bikes, and on foot, to show charity within
With glowing warmth, that can heal
It's the missionaries, with their hearts very real

24th February 2010

Choose the Right

Choose the right
Choose the right
Push temptations out of sight

Choose the left
Choose the left
Give your blessings such a lift

Choose the wrong
Choose the wrong
Pray diligently, to redeem for long

Choose the right
Choose the right
To help those, in need tonight

March 2012

Faith

Faith is a trust, you show unto others
Faith is a test, we endure with another

Faith is a hope, that comes alive
Faith is the confidence to grow in life

Faith is a dream, that becomes so real
Faith is the happiness, that we all feel

Faith is the base, the foundation to work on
Faith is the strength, that can grow inside one

Faith is a seed, planted and waiting to grow
Faith is our Father, in heaven is good to go

Faith is the assurance of things hoped for
Faith is the testimony, grown from the paw

13th September 2011

Ark

Acts of kindness, acts of love
Acts of faith, from up above
Acts of kindness, and full of heart
Acts of smiles, from the start
Acts are selfless, and are true
Acts that will help you, from feeling blue

Randomly seeking to help those in need
Randomly finding food, for all to feed
Randomly knowing, goodness is shared
Randomly seeing burdens, that need to be bared
Randomly holding all so near
Randomly showing our hopes so dear

Kindness in the heart that flows
Kindness in the light that glows
Kindness is the warm that is felt
Kindness are the smiles that are dealt
Kindness shines on the world
Kindness is a blessing untold

2nd April 2011

Thank you dear Father

Thank you Father, for the beauty in your creation
Thank you Father, for my trials and tribulations
Thank you Father, for thou wakenest me
Thank you Father, for my sight to see
Thank you Father, for blessings untold
Thank you Father, for my talents yet to unfold
Thank you Father, for my home and warmth it gives
Thank you Father, for our brother, who died, for us to live
Thank you Father, for my children and their good health
Thank you Father, for the knowledge, giving good wealth
Thank you Father, for the scriptures to read each day
Thank you Father, for the Spirit, to help show the way
Thank you Father, for my joys and sorrows
Thank you Father, for I can redeem myself against the darkest hollows
And most important, thank you Father, for you
Your timing, your work, your love, you mercy
And your faith in me

26th December 2014

Prayer of Redemption

Please excuse me Father
For my thoughts, they are not pure
Please forgive me Father
And help me to endure
Guide me from temptation's snare
For I am not without sin
Take my guilt and release me, from the lion's lair
And show me where to begin
Contemplations, that I have, now got me going
For my thoughts, they have lingered for some time
Now my actions, they have started flowing
Actions meaning I'm committing a crime
I do intend dear Father, to continue following you
But feel I need guidance, to help me follow through

Thank you Father, for your redeeming grace
And for your mercy too
For the love, you give in faith
Thank you Father, for you

8th January 2015

Our Saviour, the King

Watch me, light up, and sing
To celebrate our saviour, the king
The birth of Him at Christmas time
Brought to us, with blessings sublime

Loving and caring in cherishing others' lives
First born in a stable at midnight
The loyal, faithful, baby that was
Grew into a man, got baptised, for unto us all

Non-judgemental and grateful is He
That atoned, for our sins, blessed be
Working hard, to help pass through
The gates to heavenly Father, honest and true

At the blessed, time of year
Singing, praising and sharing cheer
Helping to celebrate, the birth of Him
Just remember, our brother, the saviour, the king

19th December 2015

S.M.I.L.E.

Spiritually Minded Is Life Eternal
Look into our hearts, and feel the hero
Hear the whispers, soft and quiet
As we gain peace, in a world of riot
See the hands, that reach out, to us near
To help and guide us, from our fear
Look to the light, where he implores
That through our prayers, we do endure
With our faith, in Him, we seek
That we're strengthened, where we are weak
Healed and comforted when we're down
Where there's a smile He bears no frown
Scriptures we read, our souls are joyful
Prayers we speak, are humble and thoughtful
And spiritually-minded is life eternal

20th October 2016

Hope

Hope is the light of life
And dreams we cannot see
And the happiness, that is felt
The sparkle shines, for you and me

Hope can bring us all together
Make our dreams come true
With laughter and love surrounding all
Hope can see us through

April 2017

Afflictions

Our afflictions are sent to us
To help us, not to control us
As we, in thee, our Father we seek
Please strengthen us, as we feel weak
Our prayers we speak, to thee above
Please help us through, and to cope
To climb high, and reach our goal
Pure in love, heart and soul
Peace be given, to us near
To uplift, the gift, from our Father dear
Thus it weakens, our afflictions
Turning to rise for better conditions

11th June 2017

Bearing your Testimony

Bearing your testimony
Is a test of your faith
The trueness of gospel
Resting warm, in your bosom's face
The light that shines
The most glorious rays
As you speak confidently
Singing His praise
Gifts, talents, and trials, we have this day
Blessings we gain, with commandments we obey
Testimonies come, when your heart is true
Of our Father, and brother too
Testimonies, bring smiles to others
As you share, and uplift one another
So next time, when you bare, your testimony
Remember, the faith you have, giving it in harmony

The Lord

When, you're feeling down
Feel, you've fallen from grace
Don't you worry
You're not in a race
Pick yourself up
Seek the Lord
He's waiting to reach out
And help you through
Embrace in the Lord
Believe in Him
He will, show your potential
If you let Him in
Open your heart
To Him, so dear
Listen to Him, very carefully
You'll be lifted, by His mercy
Love Him now, as He loves you
Your potential will, show through

9th June 2020

Holy Spirit

Be of good cheer
Let not your burdens, hold you down
Be not afraid
Seek the Lord, don't hold back

The Holy Spirit, is here today
With the rod of iron, to show the way
A witness of our Father and his Son
Foundations built, all now as one

Be blessed with courage
The potential, they see
More we learn, and don't give up
Seek to grow, never lose hope

Believe in yourself, as I believe in you
Your testimony, will grow, see you through
Visions of light, and smiles of joy
The comforter's here, oh boy

That powerful feeling, of Him so near
Gets rid, with love, of all the fear

23rd October 2020

Part 2 – Love

I'm Missing you

I'm missing you
Missing you like crazy
Without you in it
My life seems hazy
I think about you
Night and day
Wish, I could have you, by my side
Your loving arms
Surround me that way
Hold on, hold on to me tight
The warmth of your love
Comforts me, through the night
The smiles you give
The eternal glow
You are blessed
With a beautiful soul
My heart, beats fast
So I can't breathe
Thinking of you
With my weak knees
I need you, to bring me through
I'm missing, missing you

20th December 2019

I Smile

I smile, when you're here
I smile, when you're there
I smile, when you're everywhere
A breath of fresh air

I smile, when you smile
I smile, when you see
I smile, when you huddle
Up close to me

I smile, when you are happy
I smile, when you are sad
I smile, when you are lonely
I will give you, my hand

I smile, when you're frightened
I smile, when you're had
I smile, when you're angry
But don't, throw it back

I smile, when you laugh
I smile, when you cry
I smile, when you leap
So let's, take you high

Smiling is infectious
So keep it going through
Smile at, another person
And watch them, smile too

4th March 2020

I long for you

My heart, sings with joy
Your eyes, smile with hope
For every, I love you, that is said
There's a kiss, that says so
You are amazing
A cut above the rest
Your cuddles, I long for
I feel they, be the best
I'd rather be in Ireland
With you. Wrapped around me
But until then, that day comes.
I'm here, waiting for thee

12th April 2022

If I Could

You know, I'd help you, if I could
Come right to you, yes I would
Board the ferry, or fly high
To give you hugs, and kisses goodnight
Comfort you, cherish you
See you safe and warm
Cook for you, look after you
Have laughs, keep you in top form

You know, I'd be there, if I could
Experience, the life, you now love
To see the birds, in the trees
Even the ocean, at the beach
Look at the mountains, far away
In the fields of green I'll gladly stay
You know I'd be there, to help you, if I could

Your Smile

Your smile,
Is warm and affectionate
It fills me with gladness and hope
When I see you smile at me
I know that, I can cope
My soul sings, goosebumps dance
My heart, jumps with glee
For the love, that you share
And warmth, of the smile, we see
You're the rainbow to ease my pain
The sunshine, that shines bright, each day
And when I see you smiling
It takes, my breath away

11th April 2022

You touch me

You touch, my heart
You touch, my soul
You lift me up, and help me grow
A smile from you, is inspiring
Eyes twinkle bright, so enlightening
Arms so strong, warmingly surrounds
The care you give, soft on grounds
Love you share, with everyone, you know
Gives a cheery, blessed glow
You inspire me, every day
You touch me, in every way
I thank you, from the bottom, of my heart
For being there, a friend from the start

Thank you

23rd January 2019

I think about you

I think about you every day
Show concern, for you, in my way
Leave you space, that you may grow
As a friend, I love you so
You have shown, not all men, are the same
Taught me, to chase my dreams to grab, and not get away
A genuine man, yes you be
An honest friend, to me

I think about you every night
Tired and worn, in daylight
Admiring you, with a smile on my face
Of your commitments, in your height
Your priorities, you commit to
Your loving mum and daughters true
We may not talk, much right now
But as a friend, I am here, no matter how

21st October 2018

From my Heart, to your Heart

I miss you so much
I'm crying for you daily
No matter what I do
My thoughts, they precede me
I close my eyes, right beside me, you be
As your strong arms, you wrap around me
The warmth of the cuddle, that gives comfort
Delicate, is the look you give, with no effort
With your eyes, they reassure
While the smile you share
Gives peace to my heart for sure
From my heart, to your heart
I couldn't love you more

8th May 2022

The One

You're the one, what am I to do
Waking up, thinking of you
Unable to breathe, as you're not around
Yet my heart, it's pounding, so loud
Our song is playing, in my head
You're the one, is what's been said
I choke and shed a tear or two
How do I get, so near to you
Stir crazy, is what I am
You're the one, for me Tam
Missing you, I close my eyes
There you are, at my side
Giving you the biggest cuddle
Feeling warm, in the huddle
Seeing your smile, my heart pounds again
I can breathe, as you call out, my name
You're the one, again I say
As two hearts, beat, as one today

3rd March 2022

My Busy Bee

Looking at a picture, of my busy bee
The inspiration, you give me
Smiles of hope, peace and joy too
Stops me, from feeling blue

My busy bee, helping me to fly
Encouraging me, to fly high
To chase my dreams, to grab, and hold tight
Blessed be, you're an amazing sight

My busy bee, as precious, as can be
An honour, and a pleasure, to know thee
You are, a super incredible man
A star shining, since life began

My busy bee, no one, is a patch on you
You're so perfect, you shine right through
Very committed, and respectful of others
Your talents show, you're a gift, for another

3rd March 2022

We may not be Together

We may not be together
But I will forget you, never
Never thought possible, my love could be so strong
Thoughts of you, the tears that fall
My heart, it pounds, so much bigger
As my love for you, grows deeper

We may not be together
But I will love you, forever
I close my eyes, and you're there
Reaching out, to calm my despair
Every time I look at your picture
I see, an incredible man, with a great future

We may not be together
But, inspire me, you do, whatever
To reach for the stars, chase my dreams
Encourage my goals, wherever you be
No matter how far the distance
My love for you, never ceases in its existence

I grieve for you, every day
Missing you like crazy, I say
My love for you, is never-ending
Just for you, our, hearts, are binding
The love I have for you, will last forever
To the end, and even further

7th April 2022

King of my Heart

The king of my heart
We're, so far apart
Not sure, on what to do
For the king of my heart
I miss him so much
Can't help feeling blue
Across the sea
Is where he lives
In a land, I adore
My feelings so strong
Can't carry on
I have to find his door
The king of my heart
Is an amazing man
'Tis not hard, to love him so
The king of my heart
'Twas a blessing to know
His name is Tamry Groh
He touched my heart
In so many ways
Can't thank him, enough
The king of my heart
He has my heart
To live without him, 'tis tough

10th April 2022

Though you're not here

I think of you, I smile
Though you're not here
I feel you, wrap your arms, around me
And rest your head on my shoulder
I sink into my chair, as to snuggle up to you
My heart may beat harder
But feel calmer, I do
Your warm body against mine
Want to stay, like this for all time
Tender is the kiss, upon my cheek
Beautiful is the touch, that makes me weak
Completely lost in this moment
Yet I smile, when I look in your eyes
Though you're not here
You see me through
I make your dinner, as you come through the door
Taking your cap off, with a smile, I adore
Though you're not here
I know, I love you so
Though you're not here
I close my eyes, I don't have far to go
You're in my dreams night and day
When I need you the most
You're here today
My inspiration, my guiding light
Though you're not here
You're in sight

14 July 2022

I wait for you

Listening to my music
Whilst I think of you
One song starts to play
My heart breaks in two
I miss you like crazy
Maybe I'm a fool
But I can't help my feelings
My heart so all for you

I'm so lost without you
Not sure which way to turn
My love for you grows stronger
For you, 'tis whom I yearn
In your arms, I long to be
Your life I'd love to share
I would wait, for you forever
And forever, for you, be there

14th July 2022

Heart of Gold

A heart of gold, born and bred
An Irishman who has cared
Only known, for but a week
Our friendship, we hope to keep
Had already laughs, have we
Encouraged each other positively

A heart of gold, full of joy
A loving family, for this boy
Very handy with his hands
Intelligent mind, in his land
Sacrifices, he makes, for his loved ones so
Loved and respected, as a whole

Written for a great friend.
19th July 2018

That Special Person

Love of an angel
Peace of a dove
Has that special person
Smile from above
The stars that glitter, like the ocean shore
Grand is the sand, that feels smooth and pure
With the help of that special person
I've got the sun, in my hand
With the love, that's true, and very grand
The peace, the warmth and happiness to explore
That special person that I have
I shall not lose, but love forever more

2nd January 2017

A Valentine's Love

I'm into loving you so
Loving you, is simple and slow
You hold on tight, and cherish me right
More you're growing, the more I grow too
Then stronger together, me and you
You have a smile, like a sunray
Could you be more loving, no not in this day
For you to take stars, from the night
Your heart is warm, pure as daylight
Joy and laughter, like angels around
You seek the day, that comes and surrounds
Seek the person, that loves you so
Comes this day, to not let you go
Home sweet home, love lights the way
Grown from a seed, blooms right away

20th February 2016

All you need in Life

My love for you, will never waiver
It hasn't yet, it isn't either
Stronger than, was meant to be
My love for you, I truly see

I stand by you, no matter what
My heart is with, you there
No matter how, troubled you are
My soul will always care

No matter the distance, we are apart
My heart is at your side
To help you feel, the love, you want
And all you need in life

Lying down, standing up
Or sitting in my chair
I feel your arms, surround me
A cuddle from you, right there

With your head upon my shoulder
I rest my head on yours
The warmth and hope you give to me
My smile, I share for hours

Hoping one day, to be each other's guide
I will never, leave your side
The heartache I feel, not being with you
One day, will be through

30th May 2022

You are a Blessing

You are a blessing
A gift, I'm honoured to know
A pleasure, a treasure
A diamond, full of glow

You are a blessing
A very sweet treat
A cake, a chocolate
Naughty, but nice to eat

You are a blessing
A bright, sunshine ray
The rain, the snow
How beautiful, it is today

You are a blessing
In my heart so true
A brother, a sister
Sons and daughters too

A blessing to the world
A blessing to the universe
To your mum and dad too
You are a blessing
Your love and care bursts through

28th July 2019

I'd Love to Feel

I'd love to feel your body
Rub against mine
To have, your tender heart
Beat against mine
Your arms holding, me close and tight
Stops me shaking, through the night
Your lips, touching my lips
That sweet taste, just has me flip
For your hands' caressing
A gentle touch, a blessing
Your eyes, they strip me down
Now for you, I do bow

3rd March 2019

Beauty of our Love

In the beauty, of our love
like the angels, from above
Our hearts, are alight
Like fireworks, at night
The handsome man, in front of me so
Has amazing love, a pure warm glow
Supporting each other in our trials
Loving each other, giving warm smiles
As we await, what is to come
The future, we hold, in a dome
The laughs we share, and hearts we bear
Eyes to look, to see that stare
Hands that hold, gentle and soft
And lips that speak, the minds aloft
The blessings that have, come from above
It's the beauty of our love

14th June 2016

Eternally you and me

Eternally, you and me
Oh how love, can set you free
Holding each other, tight in arms
Keeping each other, safe from harm
Cherishing one another, helping each to grow
With the sun smiling, a ray of hope
Twinkling bright, are the stars at night
Hearts so warm, pure as daylight
Joys and laughter, as angels surround
The dreams and desires, of love around
Seeking for that person, to love you so
Purely, unconditionally, not allowing to let go
Home sweet home, love's lighting the way
Growing from a seed, to bloom in this day
From the love, we both desire
Eternally you and me, the love from higher

12th June 2016

You and me

I love you
You're the best
Better still, than the rest
I hold you close
Closer to me
My heart's on fire
Can't you see
My mind is wild, with thoughts and desire
Wishing you were here, taking me higher
Supporting each other, in our trials
Getting to the bottom, of the piles
Of the things, that we don't need
Things that do matter
Of course, you and me

17th February 2016

Love so True

I love you
I love you, to the moon and back
Absolutely nothing, will change that
Eternity is forever
So let's stick together, and say never
To separate lives
And unhappy ties
Meeting you, was a dream come true
Loving you, as best I can do

25th December 2015

My Valentine Just for you

To my darling Valentine, you know who you are
I didn't have the money, to buy you a fancy car
I can't afford diamonds or red roses too
All I have to offer, is my heart that loves you true
It loves you when you're sleeping, and when you're awake
I pray to God each day, that your heart, I'll never break
For that, would be too much, for my old heart to take
I know that, when you look at me, and smile at me so sweet
That you'll make me feel like, I'm in heaven and lift me off my feet
I love to make you laugh, hold you when you're blue
Wipe away your tears, and hold me, oh my sweet
Tell you that, you're my best friend and my lover too
I will love you, 'til my heart, can beat no more
And hold you close, and tenderly
To tell you that, my love for you, is for all eternity
Because my darling Valentine, my heart belongs to thee
So happy Valentine's, my darling, and to many more
I hope you have a lovely day, and all you're hoping for
But remember darling, the day is at an end
You'll always, have me, by your side
Lover, soulmate, friend

14th February 2015
By Simon Wake

Valentine

Oh Valentine, my Valentine
How would, you like, to spend the time
With hugs and kisses
Or food-filled dishes
And maybe a glass of wine

With a table for two
I so do love you
And now, Cupid has shot his darts
We have the keys to each other's hearts
To show the happiness love can bring
All our bells go ring-a-ding-ding

Happy together, happy to be
Both with contentment, everyone can see
So dear, dear Valentine, please be mine
And show, your love to me, right through time

12th February 2010

Love

Love is a gift
That faith endures
For love is pure and forever yours
With warmth you feel, and heart's real
To the tenderness, that can heal

Blessed be that love is here
The greatest gift, that's always near
Far and wide, each breath you take
Laugh with hope, in each step you make

Never give up, on love so dear
With peace and joy, there is no fear
As memories fade, in time to come
Let love, find its way, to me back home

I thank the Lord, for loving me
I bring my children, unto thee
For love holds, the very key
That opens hearts, so naturally

28th April 2009

Be with Someone

Be with someone, who will, protect your heart
Not someone, who will tear it apart
Be with someone, who will encourage, your soul
Pick it up, love it so
Not with someone, who takes advantage
Dragging you down, causing damage
Be with someone, who loves to laugh
Not someone, who rips you in half
Be with someone, who helps you, reach your goals
Not with someone, who puts, you in holes
Be with someone, who helps you strive
Not with someone, who buries you alive
Be with someone, who gives warm hugs
Not someone, who pulls the plugs
Be with someone, who has your back
Not someone, giving so much flack
Be with someone, who cherishes your stroke
Not someone, seeing you, a worthless joke
You're better than that, it's not your fault
You're not worthless, put it to a halt
Being on your own, is so much better
Than in a relationship, where, you cover for shelter

26th March 2021

If you Chance to Meet a Guy

If you chance to meet a guy
Who uplifts you, who inspires you
Don't let him go, or slip you by
For to you, he is true

If you chance to meet a guy
The man, that makes you, smile inside
His eyes that twinkle, like stars in the sky
From him, you won't hide

If you chance to meet a guy
Soul so fluffy and so light
With a heart of gold, he lifts you high
And as the sun, he shines bright

If you chance to meet a guy
Positive, in every way
Laughs and jokes, 'til you cry
Amazing man, from day to day

27th July 2018

Precious Rose

Precious Rose, pure and red
Precious rose, fully bred
Precious rose, from seed to flower
Precious rose, has the power
Precious rose, enchanted with love
Precious rose, sent from above
Precious rose, opens in daylight
Precious rose, sings with all its might
Precious rose, soft like silk to touch
Precious rose, you have given much

16th July 2018

Another you

Another month, another year
Another smile, another tear
Another winter, summer too
But there'll never be another you

Another minute, another hour
Another tree, another flower
Another dog, cat too
But there'll never be another you

Another rock, another mountain
Another water drop, another fountain
Another number, colour too
But there'll never be another you

Another book, another page
Another theatre, another stage
Another cake, chocolate too,
But, I will always, love you

29th December 2014

Into the Universe

I love you, into the universe
For, every heartbeat, that comes and goes
And every inch, of my soul, that flows
The eyes that twinkle, oh so bright
Smiles that come, from inside
Every breath, that I take
Every step, that I make
It's not my body, that is shaking
But my heart that is breaking
Thumping its way, out of my chest
To get to you, to the best
Knees knocking, at thoughts of you
With dreams, you pull me through
That one day, I will meet
The one man, I want to greet
My arms open, to your loving heart
The stars are there, from the start
To give my love, all to you
Blessed be you and me too
My heart beats forever, into the universe

4th January 2019

L is for...

Live we only do once
Let's live the best we can
Individually, or in a group
Have fun, and see, what, you began

Laughing is contagious
We share it, hopefully
With a great, sense of humour
Telling jokes, acting a silly bee

Love one another
Love yourself too
Open up your hearts
Feel the love, pass through

Life can be amazing
Embrace it, endlessly
Why not, travel the world
Or relax, by the sea

Live , laugh and love life

23rd January 2023

Part 3 – Hope

Hope

Hope is, the light of life
The dreams, we cannot see
But can, only to imagine

Hope, is the smiles, that sparkle
That happiness, that is felt
And the laughter that is shared

Hope can bring, you to me
Children, to their parents
And joy from pain

Hope is the love, that surrounds us all
The water, that flows
And nature, awakened, in the spring

Hope, is the lives, we see before us
The challenges, we hunger and strive for
And the talents, we have, become our friends

Hope is being positive, in a negative world
To grab, opportunities, that come your way
And brush away, what threatens to destroy

Hope, is the life, we have been given
The temples, for our souls
The music, that is sweet, to us all
And the sun, that shines brightly
So come on everyone, let's do this together
Let's show the world, the light of hope

21st August 2011

Positive Energy

The positive energy, you show to others
Positive beams, that shine so bright
Being around you, I know you don't cover
That encouragement, others gain from your light
You are the sunbeam, that people look to
Are kind and loving, like a sunrise
Brightens the hearts and smiles to you
The twinkle you have, shines in your eyes
Stars even sense your energy so pure
In your heart, the love you share
Your cherishing ways, could be the cure
Heart so alive, I know you'll be there
As positive energy, you have achieved
Others so low, have now been eased
Climb the hills, you inspired them too
High, above, they won't forget you

30th June 2015

Your Beauty Within

Show what it is, you want to share
All the love, and all your care
What is important, is your heart so kind
Love and hope, you may find
And when you see, the beauty you have
Hope then has, that vital chance
'Tis then, your looks, will matter no more
About your life, you can answer the door
Then the outside world, you will see
Happiness will bloom and friends will be
Will, the angels, that come to you
Shine and let your spirit come too
Through the dark, and through the light
With so much now on, you're into new heights
No more your fears, will hold you here in
Doubt not, your beauty within

Inspired by *Beauty and the Beast*
16th February 2015

Support, in your Hour of Need

In this, the time of year
The support, is here
Come to me
I give you now
My shoulders, to cry on
My ears to burn
Arms to comfort
Whenever you turn
My heart, full of love
My soul, full of joy
I hear, you call
So don't, don't cry
Eyes are twinkling
Lips are smiling
As I help, wherever I can
With no judgments, upon you
I lift your burdens
To help you through
Don't be afraid
To hold my hands
Happier days, will come again
So smile, hope, count on me
And give life a chance
My support, in your hour of need

5th November 2020

Words of Comfort (revised)

When life, seems, too much to bear
In the dark and, no one there
Feelings of distress, drives right through
Sending you crazy, and feeling blue
Frustrated with situations, at this time
Nowhere to run or to hide

Hear now, my words of comfort
To help you through, this life's discomforts
Have a break, sit right down
Take a breath, and let it out
Have some time out, for yourself
Relax to some music, have a sing as well

Release the stresses of this life
Smile again for happier times
As feathers, fall from heaven
Light has shone, now to endeavour
One day, we can, be together
All in time, night is day
You have done well just stay safe

Rewritten from first version, written back on 16th June 2010, for this time of uncertainty
7th November 2020

Don't give up

Don't give up
You will, make it
Don't give up
I have, faith in you
If you don't, give up
A chance you'll stand
If you don't give up
A success you be
If you, believe in yourself
As I believe in you
Don't give up
Stand determined
Chase your dreams
Catch them, with both hands
And hold, your dreams, tight
But don't, give, up

2nd March 2020

Never Lose Hope

Never lose hope
No matter, how bad things get
Even if you can't get out of bed
Never lose hope
When night time comes around
Dark shadows, arise, to drag you down
Never lose hope
When fear and doubt, try to change your ways
With darkness smiling, on your regretful and guilty rays
Never lose hope
When opportunity ceases to greet you
And nothing seems to go right too
Never lose hope
With you feeling low
Because you're pushed to anger's blow
Never lose hope
When loved ones are lost
Nor your dreams, can be met
Let the light of hope, shine on you
To bring you, back through
The stars that shine bright
Letting hope, be your guiding light
Holding on tight
And never lose hope
Together, we will cope

16th June 2020

Dreams

For those, who dream
And never stop
Will find their dreams, come true

For those who find
Their dreams are alive
Are happy, and content too

Having the strength
Seeing it through
Your dreams become reality

Open your heart
Have the faith
In the face, of adversity

When one dream
Has been completed
The rest are sure to follow

Then your life
Will begin to feel
Full and never hollow

24th April 2022

Sense of Humour

A good sense of humour
Is needed, this, and every day
It brings a ray of hope
For all, in every, way
Makes us laugh
And roll with glee
A gift we have
Happy to be
The world may be sour
But don't, you fret
A good sense of humour
Is what we have left
So bring on the smiles
It's what, we need
To travel, for miles
Round the world, we will succeed

1st January 2020

Happiness

Happiness is the hope of life
Where dreams are fulfilled
And you come alive

Happiness is the sunshine that smiles
And the touch you gain, like the warmth of an angel
Spreading cheer, that goes for miles

Happiness is the joys you feel
With family around, so close as can be
This contagious bug, can also heal

Happiness is the laughter, that spreads
Through strangers and friends
We'll go far ahead

Happiness is the blessing we all hold
To show unto others
The creation of life, to unfold

Happiness is such a pleasure
For all, around the world
We shall all treasure

27th August 2009

The Hero Within

The person, that cries
Is the person, who cares
The person, who cares
Is the person, who loves
For the person, who loves
Is the person, who shows patience
And with patience, comes strength
And for the strength comes courage
Then through courage, there is faith
With faith, is trust
And trust, helps with confidence
How blessed, is the person
Who has these qualities
That searches deep, into their souls
With a warm, and giving heart
To find the hero, deep within
Just, waiting to get out

12th June 2012

Smiles Through Nerves

Whenever, you feel nervous
This is what you should do
Imagine, everyone, in jester hats
And pulling, faces too

Soon your smiles begin to grow
And nerves begin to fade
Now your confidence, starts to flow
And gets its, wanted upgrade

All of a sudden, you begin to relax
Your mind begins to open its doors
Letting your words, to come out intact
And flow, right through the halls

You'll soon begin to realise
You finished, as soon as you start
Beginning to feel, mesmerised
At the words, you said, with heart

25th December 2014

Be Not Afraid

Be not afraid, to show emotion
'Tis a sign of your devotion
The strength, to keep going
Along the paths, enduring
Seeking to finish
Let not anything diminish
The spirit, so strong, you may have
A big heart too, to share a laugh
To live, to grow
To care, to show
To create memories
For the life we hold
To laugh, to cry
To love, to die
To scream and shout
To let it all out
Be not afraid, to show your emotion
It's a gift, go on and show them
Live life, be not afraid
Let the sun shine, on you today

7th October 2022

Part 4 – Inspirational and Special People Past, Present, Future

Chuck Norris

Chuck Norris, an inspiration, to us all
Motivated, is he, standing, so tall
Well known, for Walker, the Texas ranger
Watch out, bad men, you're in danger
Chuck is coming, to eat you alive
Nowhere for running, prepare to dive
Visualising, where he, wants to be
Chuck, knows, what he can see
A true legend, this beautiful man
Chuck is there, to do, what he can
Fighting, only, as a last resort
Protecting all, in his fort
Very humble, graceful, alert
Even frightens, away the dirt
How amazing, what, one man, can do
Such, as Chuck Norris, never the fool
Encouraging, others, to their full potential
A six-time world champion, super incredible
So, you see, the great, Chuck Norris
He, is the, superhero, you, are the novice

21st February 2023

Thomas

A special son, sent my way
Blessed to be his mum this day
Special times ahead it's true
For a skilled footballer, that shows through

The care he takes, with the game he loves
Is so important, with how he does
The love he shows, for his family too
Is the greatest gift, from him to you

So come on Thomas, let's grab a chair
As soon enough, you will be there
Playing football, professionally
Enjoy your games, it so can be

To my son, Thomas Michael David
30th April 2009

Love, Hope, and Faith

Loving you is unconditional
Overall
Very special
Even when I see you smile

Happy and proud, that I be
Open your heart, let us see
Plenty of love, that you may share
Enduring to show us that you care

For unto me, you were born
Amazing are you, we've sound the horn
In knowing you, I am blessed
Thank you for being my son
Happy times are the best

6th July 2022

Amy

A daughter so dear
She is so near
Free and caring
With love and cheer

A precious daughter
Who's been blessed to me
In her hour of sorrow
She comes unto thee

With her hair so blonde, she is so pure
As the gifts she gives, are the loveliest of all
But the greatest gift, that I can see
With cherish and love, it's my daughter Amy

To my daughter, Amy Wella Louise
29th April 2009

Beautiful Angel

My love for you, is unconditional
Amazing you are, I'm blessed to know
Your happiness is the smile I see
Very special, always to me
There is no limit, for the love I give
In this world that which I live
A special gift to me you are
Very beautiful, young woman by far
Precious are the memories, we may gain
With plenty more, yet to make
Like a field of dahlias planted and growing
You spread your wings, bright and glowing
So beautiful angel, I love you now
Love you forever there's no doubt

6th July 2022

Finley

Fine young man, born, into, this world
In his mum's arms, loved, so very much
Never, a dull moment, with this happy boy
Laughing and playing, with fun and joy
Every moment, is special and pure
Yet, also, precious and secure

Loving, so much, your, cheeky, smile
On, and on, it glows
Very lifting and complete
Every time, your smile flows

Never feel, you're on your own
Always here, to hold you close
No matter, how far, the distance

My love, for you, will always glisten

I love you very much
From Nan xxxx
21st February 2023

Patrick

The youngest in the family
From above and down to thee
Head to toe, like the shining sun
Stars that sparkle, when he's having fun

From the bottom of his heart
Blows his family, all apart
A smile so full, so bright can see
The love inside, so strong to his family

Scooby Doo, his cartoon caper
With family round, there is no favour
So next time, when you see a smile
Remember it's Patrick, if only for a while

To my son, Patrick Kieran Reece
30th April 2009

Just for you

Just for you
My beautiful star
A love so warm
Our beating heart

Just for you
My precious light
Unconditional love
My gift that's bright

Just for you
My cherished dove
Hand in hand
Blessed be from above

Just for you
My bright sunshine
A soul so full
It's free and flying high

6th July 2022

Our Children

Thomas, Amy, Patrick and Steph
The greatest gift, that we could get
From here, through eternity
Having fun and playing by the sea

Showing all, the talents, they have
Singing and dancing and having a laugh
Smiling so sweetly, with cheeky minds
Playing gracefully and being kind

Amy and Steph, baking for a picnic treat
Whilst Thomas and Patrick, play football in the heat
Surprise, surprise, we're going for a swim
With love from all, fun is never dim

Loving and cherishing, the children are to us
Unconditional, with heart-warming trust
With all the children, they are the best
It has to be, Thomas, Amy, Patrick and Steph

2015

Simon

His love is like an angel's light
In the sky and shining bright
With a heart full of gold
He spends his time, for you to unfold
Cherishing each moment, he has with you
Sending his stars, to you through and through

Devoted is his middle name
With his love it's not a game
Each precious touch, he gives
Tenderly, with you he lives
His smiles are forever lasting
Simon is the angel passing

19th December 2009

Stephanie

A cherished little angel
With her eyes, twinkling bright
A loving, playful, little girl
With smiles, that shine like a light

A happy little treasure
That's precious in every way
Her dancing, and her singing
Gives glad tidings every day

The energetic little jewel
Costs more than life in mind
The warmth, that's felt, from her cuddles
Are eternally divine

Her whole personality, as deep as the ocean
Such a graceful little girl that be
The warmth, and love, she has for her dad
That cherished, little girl, is Stephanie

3rd April 2010

Love Renewed, Blessings Shared

We are two stars, that shine bright
Two hearts, that beat together, day and night
A husband and wife, who love each other
Hand in hand, together forever
Committing to you, heart and soul
To continue to love, to cherish and devote
You my husband, me your wife
Two loves together, to continue our life
I love you today, I love you tomorrow
Our love we share, our hearts continue to follow

Written in August 2017 for a renewal blessing on 7th October 2017

Nan

I sit in church each week Nan
Sitting in front row, where you once sat
Waiting for the day that you'd come back
Then one Sunday, during sacrament you come
Oh how I longed, to jump up and hug you, with no refrain
Waiting so much, for church to end
So to come, sit by you and talk to you again
Tears roll down my eyes, for the happiness that you're here
Sorry Nan, I'm in your seat, but glad you are here
Smiling with pride, that you're here today
Counting down the minutes, as the sun shines bright rays
For the moment, I'm able to come hold you tight
I'm feeling sick as I can't wait, to bless you with a smile
A present from me to you to continue for a while
Thank you Nan for brightening my day
Now let me brighten yours, in the same way
I thank you now, for being my nan
Lots of love, to you I give all I can

29th May 2016

A Snowflake in our Hearts

I saw some snowflakes falling
And it seems to me
Angels coming down to greet you
To take you home
Where you're needed to be

I saw some snowflakes falling
Angels they seem to be
Collecting another angel
To help guide others
Down here, that are in need

I saw some snowflakes falling
Angels that they are
Falling softly and swiftly
Gently floating, down on me
Landing from afar

I saw a snowflake falling
An angel that you are
The angel, so soft and pure
We were blessed, to know for sure

You are our angel
A snowflake in our hearts

Dedicated to Julia Moreleigh, our nan, who sadly passed on 11th February 2017

Grandparents

Two loving people, shines like a light
A couple of angels, full of delight
With advice that, comes from them
They're our grandparents, comforting us there

Flying with wings, like doves, from above
You Nan and Grandad, are full of warmth and love
Keeping the peace and creating laughter
Having fun, playing games, here forever after

Nan and Grandad, you are, our shining stars
You reach out your hands, to guide us from afar
With your love and cherishing ways
The darkest day shines, with the sun's rays

And now, when we want, someone to go to
It's you Nan and Grandad, shining through and through
We all, love you dearly, dear Nan and Grandad
So let us, reach out to you, and give you a hand

5th June 2010

Dad

Dear, dear Dad, you are so true
How you keep me, from feeling blue
With kind, and loving words
Near or far, they can be heard

Now the best is yet to come
Dad. You're about being playful, and having fun
Hugs and kisses, all to share
A dad like you, is very rare

Being jolly, and joking all day through
And finding things, old or new
Cherishing each moment, that passes by
With your love, it sends me high

Picking up tools, to fix the sides
Doing the garden, where we can hide
Being a taxi, taking us, from A to B
The only taxi, we know to be free

I smile because, you are my dad
I laugh, as there is nothing, you can do about it
But the presents, that one had
For a dad like you, this one can't be bad

4th June 2010

Mum

A mum is like an angel, without wings
Her love for her family, is circled in a ring
The heart she has, for the children, she bore
Is nurtured, by moments, that's precious for sure

The warmth that's felt, by a mum so dear
Is cherished lovingly, for her children all near
A love that is sent from heaven on high
To show her children, the joys from the sky

The precious gift, of loving hugs
And advice that's given, comes from the heart
Unconditional, loving from, the arms of you
Dear Mum, I love you too

24th February 2010

Sheryl

A friend in need
A friend indeed
The greatest friend, that's ever been
A bright and bubbly, kind person
Giving out, a life of loving
To see her children, sons and daughters
A mother's love, never to slaughter
A friend from infants
Always to be there
To give advice, to friends who care
She takes no rubbish, and never gives up
Laughing and joking, though life is messed up
Wishing she, was far away
With her partner, and children, that play
A family, built up, by love
And friendships, all from above
The greatest gift, that's ever been given
Is a friend so dear, so I'm on a mission
Come on honey, you can do it
Joke some more, you'll get through it

November 2011

Alma

There is a special lady
Loving, kind and free
She likes to read and do puzzle books
And watch quiz shows on TV

When I go to see her
The laughs that, we both share
Just, fills, the room
Like lights, shining, from up there

She likes her scampi, and her chips too
The important things, in life to her
Are what has, pulled her through
Genuine and grateful, you will see
It's Alma, the angel, mum and friend indeed

19th August 2018

Sue

There is a lady, I have met
Bright and bubbly, and smiles shared
Won't let nothing, get her down
Keep on going, without the frown

Kind and caring, like a mum
All her friends, bound as one
With Snowdrop, her dog, in arms
Loving, cuddling, and with charm

Laughter and jokes, fill the room
Like sunlight, the blossoms bloom
The cherishing mother, that she is
The angel, I'm on about, is Sue King

18th August 2018

A Mum to One and All

You may not be, a mum to one
But you are, a mum to many
You make us smile
And show us, how to feel happy
You comfort us, console us
We feel your love, surround us
The joy you bring
To the world we're in
Has the sun shine bright above us
When the angels, hear your laughter
They sing a happy tune
For your bright and cheery ways
The angels bless you, here after
There is one thing I'd like to say
We're very blessed
To know you this day

3rd April 2019

Tamry

Tamry Groh
I give you my heart
Love it so
Tamry Groh
I give you my heart
Please, don't let it go
I love you more
Than words, could say
Trust you more
Than, each step I make
Feel you more
Every heartbeat passing
See you more
Each breath lasting
I want to
Love you, cherish you
Help you, support you
Serve you, die for you
Pick you up when you're down
Me to be, your silly clown
I miss you more
Each night and day
Never forgotten you
I have to say
Tamry Groh
I give you my heart
Love it so
Tamry Groh
I give you my heart
Please, don't, let it go

3rd March 2020

Kat

Our beautiful little Kitty Kat
Bright and bubbly, are you
Likes to colour pictures
And cuddle, teddy bears too

Our special little Kitty Kat
Loving and caring, you see
Always happy, to give a hand
And leave you laughing with glee

Our gorgeous little Kitty Kat
A busy, buzzy bumble bee
Singing joys of happiness
In all she does and sees

Our attractive little Kitty Kat
A perfect flower indeed
The kittens dance and play around
What once, was a little seed

Our perfect little Kitty Kat
In her daughter's eyes great
Such an amazing influence
That is never, filled with hate

3rd March 2021

Jacob

A loving young man. In his own way
Spontaneous in this and every day
Plays the drums, in the air
Hoping, someone is watching, him there

Loves, homemade soup, bread rolls included
Goes for long walks, listening to music
When he comes back, to sleep he goes
Then on his motorcycle, off he flows

Hates to be proven wrong, a puppy in the making
Interior decorating, hates the belly aching
Building, and making things, makes him happy
While zombie shooting, and axe-throwing, very dandy

19th August 2018

Part 5 – Nature

I Hear Nature Calling Me

I hear nature, calling me
I feel the tug, so strong
Calling me, to embrace
The warmth, of its heart, so young

I hear nature, calling me
Wrapping me up, in its bubble of calm
Feeling relaxed and tranquil
Keeping me safe from harm

I hear nature, calling me
The freedom, I now feel
That bubble wrap, nature has me in
Very blessed, that nature can heal

I hear nature, calling me
The enjoyment that I have
Fully replenished, with the love
That nature, hears me laugh

16th June 2019

Stars Twinkling Up High

Sitting, in the garden
Under, the night time sky
Looking up, at the stars
Twinkling, up high
Smiling softly, as I watch you
Just can't get enough
Of creation, I look too
The healing powers
We are blessed to have
Getting ever more relaxed
From the nature, pure like a dove
Created for us to enjoy
To embrace, to cherish
To love, and not destroy
Nothing so beautiful, in the night sky
Like stars twinkling, oh so high

24th July 2019

Hello, Nature, Hello

Hello moon, hello stars
Hello breeze, from afar
Hello rain, hello snow
Naturally, a peaceful glow
Hello rainbows, colours so bright
Hello sun, shining rays light
Hello grass, hello trees
Hello sand, hello seas
Hello bees, hello birds
Hello fish and animals, of this world
Hello spring, hello summer
Hello autumn, hello winter
Hello world, hello universe
Hello nature, created, for us

17th December 2019

I whispered

I whispered to the birds
You are free
I whispered to the trees
You're tall, I see
I whispered to the land
You are grand
I whispered to the seas
Come to me, on the sand
I whispered to the flowers
How gorgeous you are
I whispered to the grass
You will go far
I whispered to the moon, and stars
You make me smile
I whispered to the hills and mountains
I shall climb you, in a while
I whispered to all animals
Keep going, I'll be there soon
I whispered to all of nature
I love you

4th March 2020

In the Lockdown

In the lockdown
Nature, has blossomed, really well
It is looking, very swell
In the lockdown
I am a care worker, doing my rounds
One of the lucky ones, allowed out of bounds
In the lockdown
Smiling, as we are blessed
Seeing nature at its best
In the lockdown
Finally flourishing, to its fullest
Nature is at its purest
In the lockdown
Covid-19 does its worst
For, so many, it hurts
In the lockdown
Sadly, many have passed
You'll be remembered, with love ever last
In the lockdown
Covid-19, a pandemic it was
Do you realise, the loss, you have caused
In the lockdown
You've had your day
Now go, go, and stay away
In the lockdown
Life is in change
Never again to be the same

9th June 2020

Seasons of the Year

Spring, summer, autumn, winter
All the seasons, that came hither
In the spring, between March and May
Blossoms start to bloom away
The baby animals, that are born, start to take
A breath of life, in nature's wake
Easter bunnies, all go round as
Chocolate surprises, are all being found

In the summer between June and august
The summer sun, does brightly burn
As the water games, down at the beach
Blesses joy, to children's holiday treat
Then comes autumn between September and November
As nature starts to sleep again
The leaves fall, brown, orange, red and yellow
Night then falls earlier, making Halloween spooky
With ghosts and ghouls there is no rookie

Winter arrives, between December and February
The final and the starter of the year
The season of snow, that falls crisp and white
And the children, that play, with creative minds
With snowballs and snowmen and snow angels too
Christmas round the corner, children and adults all alike
Feel the excitement, then the new year flows through

11 August 2009

The Rainbow

Red, yellow, pink and green
Purple, orange and blue
Both, in the rain, and in the sun
The colours come shining through

Like a smile, the colours beam bright
In the sky, a fantastic height
For all us here, on earth to see
The colours shine, with wonder and glee

That colourful beam of light that shows
Is called a rainbow, my, how it glows
A beautiful creation, for you and me
The bands of colours, in half-moon you see

All at once, the rainbow goes
Fading, rapidly, where to, who knows
The beautiful sight, we wait anxiously
For to come again to the sky so free

16th June 2011

Nature, Beautiful Nature

Nature, nature beautiful nature
With birds in the trees, that blossomed so well
And bees, that make honey, that tastes swell
The rivers, that flow, are long and blue
The flowers, are bright, and all so new

The grass is green, buttercups yellow
Sky is blue, and colours so mellow
Come rain or shine, a rainbow shows through
And to see, that nature, is beautiful and true

As grateful I am, for the graceful creator
Who, created, this beautiful and wonderful, nature
So proud am I, for the eyes to see
The hands to feel and the ears to hear
The birds that sing, a song of cheer

In the winter, as snow starts, to fall
On mountain tops, oh how beautiful it glows
Children playing, shouting with glee
Finding pleasure, in what they see

The love, that was sought, from the Lord above
As blessings, are given, just like a dove
The love and cherishment, that's so true
The beautiful nature, sent to you

23rd January 2011

The Colours of Life

The water, dear daughter, is blue
The water, dear daughter, is blue
The poppies, are red
And the roses are too
But the water, dear daughter, is blue

The fields and trees, dear son, are green
The fields and trees, dear son, are green
The meadow is yellow
And the sun is too
But, the fields and trees, dear son, are green

The rainbow, dear Mum, has colours of plenty
The rainbow, dear Mum, has colours of plenty
The bark is brown
And the hay too
But, the rainbow, dear Mum, has colours of plenty

This paper, dear Dad, is white
This paper, dear Dad, is white
Night sky is black
And the charcoal too
But this paper, dear Dad, is white

January 2012

Magpies

Hello Mr magpie
How are you today
How are your, friends and family
Are they all out to play

Finding shiny objects
To put, into your nests
Or, finding food, for your babies
Where you can have a rest

Your black feathers, upon your back
Are as dark as the night time sky
Whilst, on your belly, are white feathers
As white, as clouds going by

On your own, or in a group
You're on the ground, so low
As in your group, we count our luck
All, coming in a row

18th September 2011

Snow

When you look, to the night time sky
So full, it looks so beautiful, so high
Soon the flakes, start to fall
Some are big, some are small
It starts to settle on the ground
The flakes join together
To form a blanket, all around
So white, and pure, just like a dove
The snow glistens, like an angel's love
Sound of crunching, the crisp white snow
And the scenery, like angels' wings
With that special glow
The hills and mountains, that are far away
Are beautiful pictures, on postcards to stay
While children, and adults alike
Make snowmen and snow angels
And have snowball fights
But for now, the fun is done, for one day
Go rest your heads, and dream of more play

16th August 2012

Dreams

Dreams you forget upon waking
Dreams are not for the taking
Dreams intrigue you
Dreams that make you go woah
Dreams confuse you
Dreams that excite you wow
Dreams frighten you
Dreams pleasure you
Dreams make you feel happy
Dreams make you feel sad
Dreams provoke thought
Dreams you actually had
Dreams telling stories
Dreams seeing the future
Dreams to help you
Dreams to save you
Dreams to look after you
Dreams to delve deeper
Look deeper to your soul
Dreams are of the subconscious
Getting you to grips with life
Dreams make you smile
Dreams make you cry
Dreams help you stay grounded
Dreams help you fly
Dreams trying to tell you something
Dreams are your guide
Dreams inspire you
Dreams uphold you
Dreams to make you feel alive

16th December 2022

The Beauty of Living

Buttercups and roses
Candyfloss and cakes
Daisies and tulips
Are beautiful, for goodness sakes
All the spring colours, are coming our way
For the summer sunshine, brightens up our day
The blossoms are open, and dancing in the breeze
Whilst in the autumn, acorns fall from the trees
In the winter, when the snow starts to fall
The blanket that has settled, sparkles, for all
Then into spring, where trees, start to bloom
Sending birds, tweeting, and happily singing to you
Oh what a blessing, of being right here
The beauty of living, has become quite clear
For the children and adults alike
Enjoy the nature, created for life

16th August 2012

Daisy

So pure, in colour, are the petals
Like the fluffy, clouds so white
The joys, of spring and summer
Sees them open wide
In the middle, is all the yellow
Representing the sun
The daisy that is here
Shows that love and life go on
The shape of the beautiful flower
Is the circle, that is formed
For, the angels, are the petals
Keeping, the family, close and sound
A family, that the angels protect
Through the night, and through the day
Keeping them, all in sight
The daisy, never, fades away

22nd June 2014

I want to go

I want to go, out in the snow
This element, gives a winter glow
The beauty, the crunch, free slushies for lunch
Head held high, mouth wide open
How many flakes, can you catch, before they're fallen

I want to go, out where blossoms bring
This element, is the element of spring
With baby animals, born, in farm and fields
Springing forward, to see what yields
When flowers, open and nature wakes

I want to go, into the sun
This element, brings warmth and summer fun
With children, and adults, down by the sea
Splashing and building, sandcastles, one two, three
Whilst on holiday, treats of ice cream and candy floss galore

I want to go, where leaves fall
This element, is the autumn call
Where a rainbow of colours, red, orange and brown
As nature goes to sleep, all over town
Then first frost, will lay on the ground

The snow, has to fall, in winter
Blossoms, to bloom, in spring
The sun, to shine in the summer
And the leaves to fall in autumn
If not, when can they, as their season ring in

2017

The Shadow

Shadow of fear
Shadow of hope
Shadow of hate
Shadow of love

Shadow of life
Shadow of death
Shadow of reality
Shadow of great depth

For the shadow, that's all around
In, the sunshine, bright and sound
Here and there, it goes with you
Dancing and moving, all the way through

For, the shadow, can be big
Or, it can be small
Like, a mirror image
It follows, stretching tall

The shadow, produces, such great shapes
Morning, noon, or evening
It's never, at all that late
Full of cheer. And laughter
The shadow makes, its break

19th September 2011

This Life a Gift

Yesterday, is history
Tomorrow, is a mystery
Today is a gift
So thank, our great Lord and Father
And humbly we'll receive, a lift

Today is called, the present
A gift we have each day
To wake with breath and life
And serve, in a fine way
Full of heart, might, mind and strength

In many a way, so different
We learn by our history
Look forward, to a mystery
And prepare for a gift
Today's present, a life on this earth

15th January 2017

Hello

Hello sunshine, bright and dandy
Hello autumn, crisp and fancy
Hello Father, very handy
Our mother too, likes her candy

Hello cold, we're wrapped up tight
Hello frost, glittering bright
Hello freshness, complete delight
Congratulations, earthly host, a beautiful sight

Hello brother, gone to wander
Hello sister tends, to ponder
Here comes winter, can't drive my Honda
It's turned bitter, the snow is at yonder

17th January 2023

Butterfly

As a butterfly
Grows, from a caterpillar
We grow, from a baby small
As a butterfly
Spreads her wings
She shows her colours in the spring
We, spread our arms, far and wide
To reach for our dreams
That stars, will not hide
As a butterfly
Dances, in the air
We dance on foot
Just to be fair
As a butterfly
Has beauty and grace
We have beauty, that we embrace

17th January 2023

Clear Night Sky

In the clear night sky
Looking to the stars, twinkling high
Seizing the chance
Some pictures, I take, at a glance
The sense of calm, feeling free
Smiles come at a great degree
Looking up to the, clear night sky
The cool fresh, night air, passes by
Such a calm and tranquil night
Fills me with, love and hope, that is bright
As I stand, with the window wide open
Feelings of the negative anxiety ocean
Drift away, how golden
Leaving behind, to the light of healing
From the darkest depths of despair
To the lightest heights of repair
In the, clear night sky

18th January 2023

Part 6 – Precious Moments

Remember Me

Remember me, with smiles and laughter
For that's the way I'll remember you all
If you can, only remember me with tears
Then don't remember, me at all

Remember, the good times, we had together
And let those memories stay forever
I am at peace, and wish the same for you
For my love, will help to see you through

Please do not be afraid
Look in your heart, your hope won't fade
Seek, for the hero, that's deep within
To find the strength, to keep you going

26th December 2014

A Baby's Laugh

Wiggle, your fingers
Wiggle your toes
I'm getting closer
And you know
Faces, I pull
Noises, I make
What I hear, when you awake
Watching you, with an eagle eye
Chuckling, like the angels, from on high
As I hear, these baby's laughs
In the presence of angels, there's no need for graft
Because of the angels, we hear today
A baby's laugh, we were blessed, in every way

12th June 2016

A Lost Angel

A beautiful daughter, born unto you
She's so grateful, and heart so true
Her family means, so much to her
A happy and bubbly, girl with cheer
Then at once, her soul is lost
The beautiful angel, gone and crossed

Learning, the words, of comfort here
To help you through, with life my dear
Your beautiful angel, you lost recently
Is at your side, to give you peace
So hold onto her, beautiful memory
Heart and soul, it's to be never-ending

As white feathers, fall gently from heaven
Hear her say, thank you now, love you forever
With words of comfort, your little angel guides
As she smiles, and shows you the light
To know, that her children, are safe and warm
Her comforting hand, will never fade, from home

6th January 2011

Wedding Day

The biggest day, of a woman's life
Is full of love, in becoming a wife
To a man, who shares, his love so strong
Cherishing and comforting her, all day long

With loved ones around, there is no doubt
That the ceremony will begin
The happy couple, make their promises
As family and friends listen in

To love and cherish, until death us do part
The vows are said, with warmth of their hearts
In this time, the wedding is done
Off to the party, that's already begun

The bride and groom, sits down, to eat
With the best man's speech, no one can beat
Both man and wife both cut the cake
Now it's time for a bit, of a shake

As photos are taken, and video recorders play
The happy couple, have the chance
To start their dance, and show everyone the way
Congratulations, to man and wife
Let your love flow, throughout, your life

5th June

Birth of a Daughter

It may not be your birthday
But, it is your day of birth
For a special gift a daughter
Was sent from above

A little angel, that's so precious
Given to parents kind and dear
The special gift of life and light
That fills hearts, so near

With love to cherish, from parents proud
The little girl, makes dreams come round
Baby you're that special precious gift
That gives everyone, a lift
Straight to the top, of the world

With joyous times, ahead with you
We celebrate, your birth so true
So welcome little one
Welcome to the world
We'll sing and dance, for you, little girl

1st February 2007

Birth of a Son

From up above and down to earth
This precious baby was sent with love
A son so little, and full of life
To give a joyful blessing, day and night

With this bouncing baby, it's true
A bundle of joy, given to you
A son you have, is born of this world
To the proud parents, who've come from above

All the days and nights, to come
This cherished son, will fill your home
With singing and dancing, as he gets older
Your talented boy will know his holders

So come and celebrate, your son's arrival
With hopes and joys, there are no rivals
Welcome into the world, little man
We'll see your face, with a smile if you can

12th July 2009

Birthdays

As your special day draws near
Let this precious time be dear
Let not one birthday pass you by
Spread the cheer as you go
One step up, the number line

Flying with happiness, and excitement too
As each year, that passes through
Treating each birthday, as your last
Celebrating you're getting older
Making it a blast

With family and friends it's so important
These exciting times, to keep a hold on
Keep treasured this precious moment
As your wishes are made
And the cake is cut

25th July 2009

To Become a Nan

Oh how grand it is, to become a nan
I'm going to be a nan, excited I am
My heart is full of smiles
My soul is full of joy
Oh how grand it is, to become a nan

Oh what a joy it is, to become a nan
I am so elated, try stop me smiling, if you can
I'm over the moon, even the stars, dance to the word
Blessed be my grandchild, that comes into this world
Oh what a joy it is, to become a nan

Oh what love is shared, in becoming a nan
When your daughter says, to you, I've got some news
You're going to be a nan
My smile fills, my heart and soul, all across the land
Oh what love is shared, in becoming a nan

Oh what dreams are made, to become a nan
A mum to be, blessed be
My beautiful daughter
Blessed with love and laughter
Oh what dreams are made, to become a nan

Thank you, Amy

23rd February to 4th March 2022

A Mother

A mother, is someone
Whose love. Knows no bounds
To be there, when you're feeling down
Wiping your tears, and sadness away
Being there for you, each and every day

She may shout, and she may scream
But she knows, her amazing beings
Whose love is unconditional
Standing proud, and standing tall
With a smile, being there, when you fall

A mother's love, is very pure
Keeping you safe and secure
She's a guiding light
That will not fade
She is there, to help you, on your way

Inspired by a friend
16th April 2020

My Heart

You say, you're shaking, you OK?
I'm fine, with a smile, I say
My heart, it's trying, to beat its way
Outta my chest, to get to you, this day
Unknown to my heart
If it knocked
I'd open the door
And let it part
From my body and into yours
Sshh, what's that sound
It's my heart, it purrs
I look deep into your eyes
You ask me again
Are you all right?
I've never been better
Smiling again
This moment, couldn't be more perfect
If I tried to catch it then
You have my heart, you have my soul
I am yours, please don't let it go

16th March 2019

As I Lay

As I lay, my head tonight
On a pillow, soft and light
I think of what
I have achieved, today
Then I smile
And drift away
My thoughts, are positive
Goals are near
I'm reaching out
With no fear
As I lay awake, next morning
Feeling refreshed
As day is dawning
My dreams are smiling
Right at me
Saying, here I am
You'll catch me, you see
As I lay, before I get up
A smile that gleams
Like a washed cup
Stars twinkling bright
Whilst around me
As I lay, and think
Of my destiny

25th January 2023

Part 7 – Thoughts, Feelings, and Experiences

My Little Angels, I'm So Sorry

If I, could do things different, I would
Let my children down. Now I'm stood
Drowning deeper, with guilt, and despair
With only, hopes, of repair
Deeper and deeper, further I go
Can't swim, or breathe, there's no flow
I just can't sleep, feeling like dross
At such a low, I'm at a loss
Forgiving myself, is to accept, what I've done
How can I do that, when their hearts, I have broken
Their mental, and emotional, wellbeing
Has been affected, what was I thinking
My beautiful children, blessed to me
My little angels. I'm so sorry

Experiences

Experiences, can pick you up
Or drag you down
But please don't frown
They are here, to help endure
Embrace them, don't fight them
Seduce them, don't fear them

Experiences, can be good, or bad
Happy or sad, or even glad
They can make you hungry, or feel full
Tired or motivated
But please. Let your experiences
Teach you, and pass you by
Then, move forward, and don't, stay behind

May/June 2018

If I Can't

How do I love others
If I can't love myself
How do I forgive others
If I can't forgive myself
How do I understand others
If I can't understand myself
How do I look after others
If I can't look after myself
How do I preach to others
If I can't listen to myself
How do I look to others
If I can't look to myself
How can I trust others
When I doubt myself
How do I be happy with others
If I can't be happy with myself
I need to listen
I need to act
I need to get motivated too
To have the faith to carry on
And trust, I can do
If I can't, I'm nothing
Nothing, without you

28th July 2019

We're Only Human

We're only human
Mistakes we make
Weakness we have
Temptations, that capture us one to another

We're only human
Emotions that we feel
Feelings that we experience
Loving others, with warmth like no other

We're only human
Every breath we take
Every step we make
And the heartbeats, that beat so pure

We're only human
Expressions we show
And tears we shed
And the smile that burns as bright as the sun

We're only human
The cultures, we live
The religion, we seek
The disabilities, we endure, in mind or physical for sure

We're only human
With thoughts and words, don't judge me
I have walked one path, a different one to you
Whilst you have walked another, that no one knows too
Words can hurt, as we're only human

11th December 2016

Hearts in Pain

Hearts open, hearts shut
Barriers down, barriers up
Staying distant, to hide the pain
As I've done, time and time again
I can't cope, with this hurt
Being invaded, by the dirt
I am suffocating, just can't breathe
These heartaches, burning really deep
In my box, these walls, surround me
Solitude coming, will be lonely
Locked up tight, so to protect
From the pain, that threats
I'm fine, I say, whilst being torn apart
Doing my crying, secretly, with my heart
Trying to hide, the pain inside
Not sure, what to do, how to act, or just ride
Into the sunset, and throw in the bucket
Or keep sane, while I rough it
Please show me, what to do
Give me someone, to talk to
And help me, for my heart's in pain
To open it up, and love again

10th and 11th February 2019

Anxiety and Depression

Anxiety and depression
The vice clamps in progression
Squeezing out, every ounce of air
From the lungs I do bear
With each breath, I struggle to gain
As I panic, with life, I remain
At a toxic low, I want to cry
Scream and shout, and just get by
I'd feel much happier, if I stay indoors
But fight to keep going, getting tired all the more
Sleep at night, what is that, I don't know
As thoughts and visions take over, I go
Deeper and deeper, I withdraw into myself
Please someone, hear my cry for help
I back into a corner, like a child so frightened
Feeling very alone, my safe place keeps me warm and enlightened
Wishing I could snap my fingers and make it disappear
Help me, get rid of this invisible disability so near
The fears I have with this disease
So debilitating, I'm without ease
Can't sit still, nothing can wait
Got to keep going, or I'll be late
I'm feeling so alone, with nowhere to go
All my burdens, a heavy weight, all out of control
Pushing loved ones further away
Cause I can't deal and cope, with my life this day
I want to be happy and be me again
So please take, this anxiety and depression without refrain

6th September 2016

Post-traumatic Stress Disorder (PTSD)

Under a thick black cloud
On a rollercoaster, to take you, back in time
Hijacked and haunted by the past
That wants to bring you down
The slightest trigger, sets your heart pumping
Right through your body, uh-oh the sweat is coming
The shakes have started, rapidly they grow
The flashbacks
Start, on the rollercoaster you go
Back to the time, that gave you the blow
Feeling sick, trembling with fear
Violently shaking, and no breathing is here
Feelings of despair, lump in my throat
Tears out of my eyes, rolling down my clothes
Can't breathe, daren't breathe
Chest so tight, frozen to the spot
Sleep is not in existence
Body in resistance
Of the pain and trauma, of the past
The experiences I lived, and threatened me
Strangles, suffocates every heartbeat passing
Shattering, every inch of my soul
Breaking and chilling me to the bone
But then I come back, to where I am now
The present, where I am safe and sound
Where my breathing takes effect
Talking myself to take a stand

When is This Trial Going to End

When is this trial going to end
This anxiety, I wish would bend
It's taken hold
It's taken grip
Holding me back
Is there no dip
Don't want to stay in
But I can't go out
Anxiety it's so debilitating, I could shout
Taking out of me all energy I own
Crippling me to the bone
I feel so tired
I feel so drained
Cause of anxiety is unknown and untamed
This anxiety is unwelcome
Though it lingers in your home
To complete its job
Of bringing you down
Laughing and crushing you at every step
'Til you sink and you drown
Giving you the harshest of blows
Just to see your all-time low
When is this going to end
I wish, I wish
That this would bend

16th December 2022

Hip, Hip, Yay

Hip, hip, yay
I managed, to do, the housework, today
Anxiety, is tiring, wearing thin
I am able, to finally, grin
Hip, hip, yay
No, panic attacks, today
Feeling chuffed, proud of myself
Four months ago, was overwhelmed
Couldn't cook, couldn't clean
Because of anxiety, cutting deep
Panic attacks, cut to the bone
Have me feeling, all alone
But, the support, that I have
Helps, to relax, smile and to laugh
To this end, I feel at a calm
Feel safe, away from harm
I, had a, laugh today
Hip, hip, yay
The dark knight, is fading, away

31st January 2023

My Life

Feeling tired, feeling blue
Must be depression, seeping through
Finding it hard, with life's demands
And feelings of incompetence, in my glands
Coping is so very hard to do
Whilst in the middle and trodden down too
By people, who didn't really care
Even those, who are meant to be there
The feelings of being alienated and withdrawn
Feeling the nerves and not being able to talk
For the faith, I have in myself and others
Along with my confidence, is far from perfect
So low am I, it's oh so true
As being the bad guy, for doing good
The loyalties, that lie are not as they should
As the people, you show trust to
Backstab and bring you down through
Their lack of interest or bully boy ways
Will have their comeuppance one of these days
Others say, revenge is sweet
Revenge for me, is living happy, my biggest treat

5th August 2011

The Metaphor

I am, as a sandwich
As the bread around the outside
Is the physical shell you see
The filling on the inside
Should be the character, you seek
Unsure of the taste
You chance to take a bite
To know the person
The character, I hide
No judgements, I make, to those around
Yet judgement, you make, are not so sound
As now the filling, you taste, and get to know
Will tell you about
The person, that is yet to grow
Past life, she has led
Has now feelings of regret
Present life in control
As she changes, her life's role
Now you know the taste of the filling
The person's character, is all about giving
The sandwich tastes, oh so sweetly
The person's life, you should cherish greatly
So please don't judge me, on what you see
Take the time, and get to know me

4th March 2014

A Banana

Like a banana
We see only, the skin
Like a banana
Our character, is within
Though, you may not like, the outside
And want to turn away
Just remember, the inside
Is different, in every way
I may be brown, and very bruised
Yuck, you may say
But if, you open me today
This, I promise you
My character, you seek, this day
Inside is what, is important
Outside is not the same
We are like a banana
Let's, not judge, each other
Give, each other, a break

16th January 2023

Frightened

Frightened of being happy
Frightened of getting close
Frightened of loving others
And giving of the most
Frightened of asking for help
That's needed so desperately
Frightened of those around my life
That walk all over me
Frightened of talking about my feelings
In case of being judged
Frightened of coping by myself
Although through my life I have
Frightened of having fun
In case of a grilling
Frightened of being comfortable with myself
Without feeling I'm an ugly duckling
Frightened of saying no, or giving my opinion
As I'm guilt-tripped, into taking back
Everything I believe in

14th May 2012

A Broken Heart

To give your heart, to someone you love
Is very easy to do
But then things, start to go wrong
They break your heart in two

They stand you up, and break you down
And smash your heart to pieces
The feelings then that follow
Are black and gloomy, leaving you in dark places

Your heart cries out, it wants to be fixed
But no one's there to do it
As mourning your heart, that's lost and broken
And finding that special person to fix it

The motivation, that you once had
Is just a distant memory
For the love, that's left, that broken heart
Has left you numb and empty

30th September 2011

Forgiveness

Forgiveness is an amazing thing
With your strength and love within
For those, who go against you
Your love for them, will guide you through

Being graceful with your actions
Seeing through others, and their distraction
The way, they treat you, is no fun
Befriending and then backstabbing, then go on the run

Using you, for they don't care
For what they can get, from you out there
Starting rumours, that are not true
Turning all others against you

Laughing and joking, putting you down
With confidence and strength touching the ground
For the bullies, who think they've won
But they don't realise, that you are the one

That shows your love, that is within
For forgiving them, is an amazing thing

20th October 2011

Soul-searching

Feeling anger, feeling pain
Feeling the tears, and going insane
Such a difficult thing to do
To control, the feelings, that flow right through
As you go, into your past so deep
So to understand, your soul so grieved
Then I have them burning questions
Who am I, why am I here
Wanting so much, to shout out loud
But my voice is covered, with a thick grey cloud
The thing, called soul-searching, is what it's called
Oh so very hard, please help me I'm flawed
So many memories, that come unto me
Just takes me back, with anguish indeed
Too frightened to continue
For that, same loop, I may, have to go through
But to pluck up the courage and follow with strength
You can fight it, to the end
Then soon, with a smile, and your soul relieved
You know who you are, and it feels like a treat

14th and 15th August 2012

Poverty

Living in poverty and living on the line
No food to eat, nor money to dine
Scrimping and scraping and saving every penny you can
To get a slice of bread and milk warmed in a pan

Children have, no toys to play
And parents battle, to keep them at bay
Struggling to pay, the high rising bills
With fear of eviction, and going green at the gills

Choices they can't have, is too much to bear
Where's the next penny, for a meal, where
No water in taps, for those to bathe
No heating in the home, to heat another day

At wit's end and living above their means
No time for family life, no time to breathe
Nowhere to go, nowhere to hide
As ill health rises, with hard work, just to survive

No eating or sleeping, as they've gone astray
As worries of choices may, have children taken away
Aggravated as can't celebrate, special occasions
Painstakingly gruelling, now giving up on salvation

28th December 2014

Stronger than Life

I needed you, but you weren't there
I was alone, but you didn't care
I was depressed, you didn't support
I needed your help, but shouting was for nought
You just laughed, as you mocked
You didn't listen, and thought you rocked
No love, or appreciation, you gave
Your love I needed, that I might stay
Yes I loved you, but you broke my heart
Encouragement to others, that tore me apart
Emotionally, physically, mentally drained
But you just laughed at what you gained
The words and actions you did so
Left me less and less with hope
As your, arrogant ways, did cause harm
I stayed silent, for the sake of calm
With my words, you did not take heed
Now no more, do you have me
Stronger than life, I now live
All my love, I shall now give

The Negative Life

The feeling, of suffocation
This life, that holds me back
As the negative, environment I'm in
Stopping me, and there's no slack
I scream, and I shout
But my voice, it can't be heard
As no one is about
Where are they all, it's all so blurred
Positive, is the energy I crave
someone, please come unto me
so desperately I want to save
that positive feeling, please let it be
the support I'd like, but cannot get
my tears are drying up too
the positive energy, please bring me I beg
I want to laugh and act a fool
Please help me, help those in need
And brighten up their lives
Just to plant, that little seed
And nurture them, in positive sunlight
The negative life, I so don't want
And the positive, I so do
So turn away, the dark clouds fast
And bring my sunshine through

3rd April 2015

Fantasies

Fantasies, they should stay
As where to, they lay
With the problems, they can cause
Trouble and strife and unclosed doors

Letting them loose, has riots begin
Stronger than thought, reeling you in
Feelings that grow, sets you a light
Reality seeps in now you can't fight

Struggling with your mind's desire
Your heart, is burning, like it's on fire
Wishing that it would stop
Reality goes from cold to hot

Fantasies are what they say
Let them stay, where meant to lay
Keep those doors locked, throw away the key
Lose the thoughts, strike them and flee

3rd June 2016

Feeling Alone

Feeling alone, in the dead of night
Gasping for breath, my chest feels tight
I can't breathe, though try as I might
Feeling alone, and feel I'm in a fight

I just can't sleep, it's doing me in
Partner says, see you in a bit, then gets sleeping
Lying back down to sleep, he starts snoring
I understand, he has work, in the morning
But this is a joke, I can't take this unsupporting

I feel all alone breathless and in pain
Wrapped in my blanket, in aid to gain
The comfort and cuddles, to keep me sane
I feel like crying, I'm so drained

Shaking my head, can't believe, that I must
Deal with this, in the night time dust
Whilst others get their lifetime lust
I'm feeling alone, and all out of love

Selfish, as it may sound, but that is as it is
That's the way life goes, even in the abyss
So now, I take comfort, in my blankets warm
To try, get some sleep, hopefully 'till morn

23rd February 2016

Grass is Greener

They say the grass is greener, on the other side
But if you look deeper, you may just find
Burnt brown patches, where the sun has lay
And no water sprayed, upon the grass that day

They say the grass is greener, very tempted too
To go to the other side, and start all anew
Moving to the other side, you know not about
Thinking you know everything, and wanting right back out

They say the grass is greener, now this feeling's fled
The bad decisions, that you made, you now regret
Wishing for the new life, has brought nothing but trouble
Now it has collapsed, you're sorting through the rubble

They say the grass is greener, but it's not true
The greener grass is where to stand, if only you knew
The life it is that you now have
Is a blessing, sent to you, so gratefully have a laugh

I say, the grass is greener, only where you stand
Past decisions, and mistakes made, are all in your hand
Next time, when you look, at the other side and see the grass so green
Have the courage, to stay where you are, and enjoy your life humbly

22nd May 2017

Be Careful What You Wish For

Be careful, what you wish for
Or bite your bum, it will
Words that are spoken of
Will haunt you, forever still
Wishing is a dangerous game
Especially for ourselves
Thoughts going around our heads
With our minds, they do swell
Sometimes wishes are for the better
And sometimes, for the worse
But in cases, for the latter
Your life continues as dross

28th May 2017

It's Not Your Fault

It's not your fault
Most men are the same
You're a pawn, in their cruel game
A piece of meat, to pick up and drop
A joke too far, takes pleasure in the mock
Mentally, emotionally, physically or verbally
Dragging you down, taking away your dignity
Soon the confidence and self-esteem
Shows no sign, and you start to dream
You know not, on what to do
To break free, or live in gloom
As the abuse, continues behind closed doors
And also in public, in the outdoors
With their name-calling, and their demands
You're too frightened, to stand your ground
Stopping you from, what you want to do
Who you call, and who you talk to
Believe in this, it's not the way to live
To experience this in life, it's not your fault
Get out, as soon as you can, and ground it to a halt

27th February 2018

Look for the Hero

Look for the hero, deep within
Deep down inside, the fighter begins
With the strength, of a lion
In times of your trial
You're seizing the moment
Heart and soul on fire
And the courage that comes
Feeling the desire
The fight to go on
Fighter's instincts to get where you want
Growing and growing
Stronger than ever
Each, in their own individual ways
Day after day looking deeper
For the hero, that is within
You can be who you want to be

April 2018

Cancer

Cancer is like a demon
Apply destruction, with no, discrimination
Nagging at the organs, to bring them down
Creating havoc, with no mercy, no frown
Erupting through your body's hull
Raging just like a bull

Treating this bully
Reaching to its core
Entrusting full power
And pushing it, out the door
Tenterhooks, are feelings, there
Management, with those who care
Enlisting those, all about
Now the anticipation, of the result
Time is here, the treatment is done
See what's coming, it's not fun

28th April 2021

Homeless

I am a human being
With emotions, and yes feelings
Can't someone, give me a hand
I don't bite, but I live in this land
Yes I'm homeless, but I'm like you
Only difference is, I have no roof
No clothes, but what I wear
No food, I wish was there
Every night, I get so cold
No money, to get blankets of old
To keep me warm, and somewhat secure
Knowing not, to what I endure
You treat me, like, I'm beneath you all
Just because, I had that fall
My life's path, has been unfortunate
Doesn't mean, that it was my fault
Life's mishaps, can happen to anyone
So please I ask, don't ignore me, and walk on
Thank you, to the one, that does give
Blessed be, for the gift

11th June 2021

I Used to be Frightened

I used to be frightened, being alone
No one to love, being on my own
Fear of isolation, and being, left on the shelf
To have no one, but only myself

Once I was scared, I did silly things
To get attention, and everything it brings
Wanted so much, for my life to share
With someone, I thought, would be there

Second best I did settle
Just to get, one in the saddle
Hoping I'd have, someone to care
How wrong I was, I now declare

Unsure as to why, I feared being alone
Perhaps, maybe, it was the unknown
Going into, the big wide world
Out of the bubble, secure and furled

Now I'm changed, through experiences undesired
Much better on own, I'm even inspired
I've no need, to be afraid
Happy, content, solo I'll stay

9th May 2021

I Remember When

I remember when, at Christmas
We raced, to our, Christmas presents
Our camping trips, in summer
Were full of presence

I remember when, at my nan's
An onion, I hid
But to this day
Not sure, where I put it

I remember when, my exam results
I felt, weren't good enough
Yet, I smiled
As they were, quite tough

I remember when, feeling so worthless
Because of judgements, from others
But that was then, this is now
Life is different, for me, see how

Anger

Anger is an emotion, that builds up inside
Not a good thing, and it cannot hide
As people, you thought, you could trust
Tread you down and accuse you of trouble
The adrenaline, starts to pump, and blood boils
You find, your head, soon messed up, and in toil
You want, to lash out, but can't get enough
Of the fuel, that has you explode, it's so tough
Then at last, you start to strike out
Shouting, and balling, without a doubt
Fists fly, your feet do too
Now the tears, you have start to flow through
As the adrenaline, starts to slow down
You feel yourself, coming around
To the sun, that shines so brightly
And you, start to smile
As now, the anger has gone, for a while
My advice, to save unwanted regrets
Is, to be, slow to anger, that is the best

31st August 2011

The Poem of Love

Please bring to reality
The love I wish for
The love I'd like
Bring him near, so we may find
Our love so strong, with caring minds
The loving feeling, that we may feel
With honesty and warmth, that is so real
Understanding, that we both, can see
Holding each other, so naturally
Helping our hearts, to bind as one
That we may live, forever long
The dreams, that come true
With love, to see us, through and through
As tender as the touch, like a new-born baby
Forever together, from here and through eternity

12th July 2009

Part 8 – Inspirational

Inspiration

When your thoughts that proceed
And your mind is so in need
For the mind, that wants to uncover
Creativity to show for another

With passions flaring, talents fly
The power that comes from on high
Helps the way, for you to see
What you create, so diligently

For the angels, that guide you so
To the light, which shines, and shows you how
The passion that helped, for you to create
An expression, which is never too late

19th July 2009

You are Blessed

To have the outdoor beauty
With the sight to see
You are blessed, to be able to hear
With family close and dear
You are blessed, to have life and breath
With a roof over your head
You are blessed
To get into, a warm bed
With love, gratitude and mercy said
You are blessed
To smile, laugh and have joy
With the ones you love
You are blessed
To own one of the gifts
Or even more that lifts
You are blessed, and very rich

9th January 2021

Talents

Use it, or lose it
Your talents are precious
Given as gifts
Talents, to share, with others
To guide them through, their days
Help others, to grow in life
Inspire them to chase their dreams
And hold onto them tight
Make your talents shine
Dreams to sparkle bright
Come in, and unfold
True talents are in sight

1st December 2019

Bonfire Night

Remember, remember, the fifth of November
As fireworks, in height, light up the sky
Guy Fawkes then waves, his last wave goodbye
With smiles on faces, and people take their places
To watch the fireworks, as the fire blazes

Wizz bang, scream bang, go the fireworks
Twizzing, whizzing, up they go
With fabulous colours, the fireworks blow
Now the fire starts to shrink
Like shooting stars, you dare not blink

Bonfire night comes, once a year
So please be careful, don't shed a tear
Thanks for listening, I'm almost done
Now let's go, and have more fun

With sizzling hot dogs, in their bread rolls
At the fairground, you're on your toes
The rides, that all, surround you here
With your families, you stay quite near
Now, it's time, to say goodnight
To wait, another year, it's quite alright

Written by Amy Barnes (my daughter, aged 13 years)
28th October 2010

The Two Wolves

Two wolves, fighting
In the field, they be
One of doubt, regret and greed
And one of, love, hope and patience, you see
Waiting, for their food, to come
Both in a state of hunger
Fighting 'til, their hearts' content
Just to see, who's stronger
Now the food, has been given
Who's the first to eat
Love and hope got there first
Doubt and regret, was beat

(The wolf you feed, is the wolf that wins)
2nd March 2020

I Started Reading a Book Today

I started reading a book today
Little did I know
How very quick, and interested, I became
The further, into it, I go

I started reading a book today
Much to my surprise
Once, I had no patience, to read
Now I'm on the rise

I started reading a book today
More interesting it seems
The internet, and TV
Are no entertainment for me

I finished reading a book today
Most tearful, I did get
A good book, that I read
This really, I shall not forget

2nd February 2017

Merry Christmas

Mrs Santa, has come to say
Merry Christmas
Have a great day
The presents given unto you
With love and thoughts, sent on through
Sharing smiles
That go, for miles
Love to one, and love to all
This time of year, your heart's a-glow
With happy faces
And glowing graces
Merry Christmas, enjoy your hols

25th December 2015

Racism

There is a place, for you and me
It's here on earth, where the eyes of hate, can't see
For the heart, that's unable to feel
The soul sorrowful, and grieved, it's unreal
Because the heart, is hardened and so cold
The unkindness spreads, and gets a hold
Through the jealousy, one feels for another
Of the origin unknown, and yet to discover
Feeling like an alien, shoved in the cupboard
Trapped and isolated, with nothing covered
Black, white, red, green or blue
All curled up, with racism, what's there to do
Please, please, stop picking on me
It's not very clever, as you can see
Hurting others, with your blind and selfish ways
Will get you, put away, one of these days
So now, the advice, I give the world, and its universe
Please give others, the respect, they deserve

10th September 2011

Happy New Year

Hours of happy times, with family and friends
Abundant time, for relaxation
Prosperity and revelation
Plenty of love, when you need it the most
Youthful excitement, at life's simple pleasures

Nights of restful slumber
Everything you need
Wishing you love and light

Years and years of, good health
Enjoyment and mirth
Angels to, watch over you
Remembrances, of family, in the new year through

January 2012

Christmas

Christmastime is here again
It comes but once a year
For children get, excited to open
The presents they have with cheer
As the presents they have are opened
One by one, paper is ripped
For as this, a special time
You play a game of lucky dip
You dip into your Christmas sack
With only thoughts of fun
To find, the presents they wanted, are number one
Then comes lunchtime, a special treat
With turkey on the table, you'll be eating the next two weeks
Christmastime, is a time for giving
And celebrating a special birth
Many, many a year ago, Jesus was born unto this earth
Remember, remember, Christ is here
With all His love, and plenty of cheer
Now I'm finished, it's time to say
Happy Christmas, and New Year, unto this day

16th November 2009

Easter

On this special Easter weekend
We celebrate, our brother, who died and rose again
A special man, born unto this world
Is as pure, as the newly, fallen snow
To show His long and everlasting love
On Good Friday, He attoned and crucified, to save our souls
Then on the third day, we call Easter Sunday
Jesus Christ, did rise again
Then ascended, to our Father, up in heaven
In this time, we celebrate, this day
To thank our Father and brother above
The righteous path, they've shown us with love
The treats we have to celebrate this occasion
Are the chocolate eggs, to share, for the life and love given

2nd April 2010

Thank You

There is a word, I'd like to say
From me to you, in a positive way
This word is heartfelt, and is cherished
So divine and full of love, it won't be perished
It's a little word, with a very big heart
Which said unto you, can make you smart

This word that I give you
To brighten the darkest day
Is for the help, that you gave me
The time you shared, diligently
To help me move, from A to B
The gratitude, I have, will be seen

Now I give you, the word so bright
That has the sun, smile through the night
So heartfelt, and welcome true
Cherished and loved, through and through
So from the bottom of my heart
I say thank you, from the start

Thank you

8th November 2009

Football

Football, is always coming
Round and round, up and down
Going and going, on and on
Everybody's always, coming and turning
To score a goal, and hear the audience cheering
Now it's nobody, is really not stunning
West Bromwich Albion, is so the best
I can't stand, they're beating the guests
Hurray, yippee, West Brom has won
Now that's, the end of the game
Football is now done

Written by Patrick Barnes (my son, aged 6 years)
25th February 2010

Charity

There are bright and cheery minds
Full of heart, and love divine
Charity brings, with helping hands
Warmth and tenderness, in the lands

Caring holds a joyful praise
And happiness, that will fulfil the days
Helping souls, into their hour
To see them through, their lives so sour

With those willing hearts we bind
And charity round, that we may find
Peace and joy, and warmth too
And happiness in society, will show through

20th July 2009

Happiness is

Happiness is, about being, not having
Appreciating yourself, and laughing
Providing self, with comfort, and care
Pushing self higher, with no despair
Introducing trueness, to self, to employ
Nourishing yourself, with gladness and joy
Encouragement to self, to reach goals and dreams
Strong sense of worth, to self that gleams
Stick to the positive, and enjoy, being you
Important to say, you will get through
So don't delay, your happiness, is truth

3rd March 2021

Let Your Inner Child Out

Let your inner child out
Let her play, let her shout
Sing, dance, play a merry game
Splash in puddles, in the rain
On the swings, down the slide
Fear not, we're going for a ride
Let your fears all drift away
Like a child, in each day
Laughing and smiling
Falling and rising
You inner child, is free again
Free as a bird, to live, not lay
Have as much fun, as you can
Young or old, there's no ban
Go for a skydive or climb a wall
Make sandcastles. Build them tall
Get dressed up, shout out loud
Let your inner child out

1st December 2019

Individual Happiness

Our individual happiness
Is a blessing
Don't take it for granted
It is your dressing
To rely on others, for your happiness
It just will not do
You need your happiness
To guide you through

Your individual happiness
Is of importance in life
Look deep for the hero within
Go give it a try
If you're not happy
Then do what you will
Find yourself
Embrace the thrill

Climb the mountain
To find what's true
Seek the Lord
And I'll meet you there too
Encourage your happiness
To be free
We will have fun
You wait and see

4th September 2020

Lisa

L is for her tenderness, the sweetest kiss, her gentle breath
The way she loves and holds me close
I know she's the most amazing person, I'll ever get to know
And in my heart, I know, I just can't let go

I is for her eyes, the way she looks at me with big surprise
As I tell her, how I love her so, and I know, that her love
For me is very pure, and she will love me, this I'm sure
As we are one and meant to be, I know she is my destiny

S is for sensitivity, how she sees the good in me, and when
She holds me tenderly, and never to let go, it makes me care
So endlessly, and she will always know, she believes in me
To be there to comfort her so

A is for adorable, for all she does, in her sweet life
The way she helps, and embraces life, I'm a lucky man
I was sent an amazing person, for me to love
I know that in my heart, we are meant to be
From here to eternity

Written by my husband, Simon
2nd March

Words of Comfort

When life seems too much to bear
In the dark and no one there
Feelings of sorrow, that drive right through
Sending you crazy and feeling blue
Frustrated with your life's demands
No appreciation, and no thanks

Hear now the words of comfort
To help you through, with life's discomforts
Have a break, and sit right down
See the sunshine, bright and round
Relaxing, to some peaceful music
Surrounding yourself, with grace and light

As white feathers fall gently from heaven
Your prayers be answered, with glory forever
With words of comfort, your angels guide
Singing and dancing, and showing you light
All at once, the night is day
The angels' guidance, have shown you the way

16th June 2010

Paradise is Not a Place

Paradise is not a place
But it is a feeling
A place you're in, you embrace
With people, to help, your healing

Paradise is not a place
But a state of mind
The joys and laughter, all with grace
And the warmth, that is inside

Paradise is not a place
But a sense of direction
The heart that beats, at a pace
And the smile endures, great sensation

Paradise is not a place
But a goal to work to
Happiness and love, will trace
To the path, you walk through

1st December 2019

An Old Man Staring Back at Me

Today, I looked into the mirror
And what did I see
An old man staring back at me
As I stood, I remembered
All the things I wanted to be
I remembered as a child
Being young and carefree
The dreams of being a pilot
Or a captain at sea
But, a father, I would certainly be
I'll never be rich, I'll never be poor
And my children, couldn't inspire me more
To be kind, and true to others
And be the best I can be
To remember fondly
All the good times in my life
So glad you're here, as my wife
The wasted moments I have had
Doing nothing, throwing away potential, my lad
But I am happy as can be
When I looked into the mirror
And saw an old man staring back a me

6th December 2016

Man in the Moon

Man in the moon, smiling down on me
Man in the moon, shining for all to see
A hero at night, to all who roam
With a natural, night light, that he brings
Through the windows, shining, for me at home

Waving in, the night time hours
Sending to sleep, the beautiful flowers
Bigger and brighter, the rare supermoon grows
Man in the moon, getting closer and closer
Oh how it shows, within him, as he glows

So next time when you see the moon
Remember the man, shining, and waving at you

15th January 2017

Part 9 – Personal and Favourites Written

Unique Me Unique You

This is me, I am one
There is only one as unique as me
Uniquely individual, you can see
My disabilities, my strengths, my weaknesses too
Makes me unique, in my individual way, cool
My flaws, my experience, my mistakes, my character
My religion, my life, my colour, my fun-factor
This is what, makes me, me
The one and only, unique individual me

This is you, you are one
There is only one as unique as you
Uniquely individual, I can see
Your disabilities, your strengths, your weaknesses too
Makes you unique, in your individual way, cool
Your flaws, your experience, your mistakes, your character
Makes you completely different, even your fun-factor
This is what makes you, you
The one and only, individual unique you

Everyone is different, in their individual ways
Everyone is special, in their own unique way
Unique me, unique you
Unique individuals, through and through

April 2018

What Christmas Means to Me

What is Christmas, but love and harmony
What is Christmas, but friends and family
Not just the presents, under the tree
This is what Christmas, means to me
The Saviour was born, in a manger bare
Surrounded by the people, who looked on with care
Mother Mary, Father Joseph, Angel Gabriel too
Three wise kings and the shepherds, cool
With gifts by His bed, peace in His heart
Jesus was happy, right from the start
No tears did He shed
Only smiles from His bed
This is what, Christmas means to me
Love hope and charity
Every Christmas we celebrate the birth
Of the king, who saved us, on earth
We gather together, family and friends
Creating peace, calm and tranquil end
It's not the presents, we give, under the tree
But it is, what Christmas, means to me

20th December 2022

Ireland

The beauty of Ireland, and its shore
With trees and flowers and buildings galore
Beautiful fields and sights to see
Can't resist the accent, phwoar, please teach me
I'd like to live, there one day
Very peaceful, and calming, I must say
Extremely musical, that I love
Touching the hearts of others, like a dove
Dreaming of such beauty, where I long to be
Where great people, welcome thee

6th September 2016

An Irish

An Irish proverb
An Irish prayer
Lifting me, right up there
An Irish blessing
An Irish smile
Taking me, to more miles
An Irish song
An Irish dance
Here you are, here's your chance
An Irish home
An Irish heart
Just to say, we're never, far apart
An Irish Craic
An Irish humour
A lot of fun, that's no rumour
An Irish language
An Irish scenery
Very beautiful, blessed be

3rd March 2021

I'd Rather be in Ireland

I'd rather be in Ireland
'Tis where I'm meant to be
Ireland is where, I feel at home
And where, I feel free
Breath-taking scenery, to take me back
The joy, the fun, and the craic
Steeped in history, to go explore
A beautiful island, to love and adore
To work and live there, would be an honour
My feeling homesick, would be a goner
Never lived in Ireland, neither was I born
But a call, from that sweet place
To my heart, is loving and warm
Happy and content, is what, I long to be
Here in England, is not the life for me
I'd rather be in Ireland
'Tis where I'm meant to be

12th April 2022

My Children Mean the Universe to Me

My children mean, the universe to me
Although others may decline to see
I have my flaws, and made mistakes
But this I cannot lie
I love them all so dearly
And very proud of them too
My children mean, the universe to me
I think they're really cool

My children mean, the universe to me
They're very wise indeed
They are learning, more each day
I know, they will succeed
Whilst I give them, my advice
On experiences, I have had
My children mean, the universe to me
I'm blessed to be their guide

My children mean, the universe to me
They have come, a long way
I know decisions, they may make
Will see them through each day
Surrounded by their family and friends
They laugh and have fun
My children mean, the universe to me
So come join with me, and never be done

1st July 2015

Hope

Hope is, the light of life
The dreams, we cannot see
And the happiness, that is felt
The sparkle shines, for you and for me

Hope can bring us, all together
Make our dreams, come true
With laughter and love, surrounding all
Hope can see us through

April 2017

www.ingramcontent.com/pod-product-compliance
Lightning Source LLC
Chambersburg PA
CBHW022103090426
42743CB00008B/702